D1291158

DATE DUE

UNCERTAIN
RESURRECTION

GAYLORD   PRINTED IN U.S.A.

By the same author
WHITE REFLECTIONS ON BLACK POWER

UNCERTAIN RESURRECTION

The Poor People's Washington Campaign

by
CHARLES FAGER

William B. Eerdmans Publishing Company
Grand Rapids, Michigan

D

©Copyright 1969 by William B. Eerdmans Publishing Company
All rights reserved
Library of Congress Catalog Card Number: 78-75101
Printed in the United States of America

This essay is for
MORRIS MITCHELL
Founder and Director of Friends World College
and for
WILLIAM E. MORGAN
President of Colorado State University, 1949-1969

PREFACE

This account is one result of an effort called the Poor People's Documentary, in which the writer was a participant. My colleagues in the project were Letitia Hastings Fager, Larry Frank, Krystyna Neuman, Steve Raitt and Henry Wilhelm, to all of whom I am greatly indebted for gathering and interpreting a mass of information beyond what I was able to get on my own. The Documentary was made possible through the generous and nondirective assistance of a number of people, especially Mr. and Mrs. John Raitt, Mrs. Helen Raitt, Mrs. Lois Hogle, Miss Susan Kaeser, Mrs. Jane Gilmer Wilhelm, and not least the administration of Friends World College. Special notes of appreciation are due Mr. William B. Eerdmans, Jr., my patient and progressive publisher; Dr. Albert Gollin of the Bureau of Social Science Research, who kindly took the time to give me the benefit of his informed scholarly criticism; and Miss Carol Browne, who for a number of reasons deserves more recompense than these few words can convey.

A Note On Sources

The materials assembled and interpreted in the preparation of this account included the following: some thirty tape recordings of an average 90-minute length; daily perusal and clippings of *The New York Times, The Washington Post, The Evening Star, The Washington Daily News,* and *The Christian Science Monitor;* several thousand photographs taken during extended travels across the Campaign's various caravan routes; and direct observation and interviewing by myself and my colleagues during the weeks from May to August, 1968, the period of the Campaign's action phases. Footnotes have been avoided by incorporating the

7

necessary citations of date and source into the text. A consistent effort has been made to differentiate between what the writer regards as matters of established fact and his interpretations or surmises regarding such facts. The former, where not noted otherwise, are based on direct observation, supplemented occasionally by careful reconciliation of the various journalistic accounts.

In any social movement on the scale of the Poor People's Campaign there are a multitude of things going on behind the scenes, some of them of possibly greater significance than many visible developments. From our vantage point as independent interpretive journalists, most of these maneuverings were not directly perceptible. No doubt the Campaign's moldy cadaver will eventually be exhumed and exhaustively dissected by a corps of PhD candidates, and its inner secrets will be exposed. While the results of this post-mortem will surely refine and correct much of the present account, the writer remains cautiously confident that they will bear out its substance and conclusions.

– C.E.F.

Harvard University Divinity School
April 30, 1969

CONTENTS

Revolutionary Letters #19, Diane DiPrima

if what you want is jobs
for everyone, you are still the enemy,
you have not thought thru, clearly
what it means

if what you want is housing,
industry
    (G. E. on the Navaho
    reservation)
a car for everyone, garage, refrigerator,
TV, more plumbing, scientific
freeways, you are still
the enemy, you have chosen
to sacrifice the planet for a few years of some
science fiction utopia, if what you want
still is, or can be, schools
where all our kids are pushed into one shape, are taught
it's better to be "American" than black
or Indian, or Jap, or PR, where Dick
and Jane become and are the dream, do you
look like Dick's father, don't you think your kid
secretly wishes you did

if what you want
is clinics where the AMA
can feed you pills to keep you weak, or sterile,
shoot germs into your kids, while Merck & Co.
grows richer

if you want
free psychiatric help for everyone
so that the shrinks,
pimps for this decadence, can make
it flower for us, if you want
if you still want a piece
a small piece of suburbia, green lawn
laid down by the square foot
color TV, whose radiant energy
kills brain cells, whose subliminal ads
brainwash your children, have taken over
your dreams

degrees from universities which are nothing
more than slum landlords, festering sinks
of lies, so you too can go forth
and lie to others on some greeny campus

THEN YOU ARE STILL
THE ENEMY, *you are selling*
yourself short, remember
you can have what you ask for, ask for
everything

1

A Last Desperate Demand

During the last two years of his life, events — chiefly the Vietnam War and the related tides of black militancy and ghetto uprisings — seemed to conspire to drive Dr. Martin Luther King, Jr. leftward. Dr. King moved left with considerable reluctance, for his was a conservative personality, at home in the largely white liberal elite of which his achievements had made him a pillar and from which he drew substantial support. The statements of such elite opinion-makers as *The New York Times* made clear to him that association with antiwar protests or the black militants would threaten his position in this "establishment." And for more than a year after the bombing of North Vietnam began, Dr. King was virtually silent on the war and hostile to those whose quest found its slogan in Black Power.

Yet the passage of time ultimately made these positions intolerable, to both his conscience and self-interest. Support for the war was made the condition of continued favor with the Johnson administration even as the Great Society's domestic programs were being decimated to finance it. Dr. King's Christian pacifist convictions, moreover, were outraged by the increasing and evident horror that was America at war. The urban uprisings forced him into embarrassing, almost Uncle-Tomish statements, such as the one supporting the sending of federal troops into Detroit in July, 1967. These

13

positions played into the hands of militants trying, with alarming success especially among the young, to discredit him in the ghettos. Such developments were beginning to dilute his credibility among black people and cast a threatening shadow on his power base. At the same time the uprisings brought home to Dr. King the shallowness of the earlier nonviolent victories, showing unmistakably how little they had improved the day-to-day lot of most black people.

After a long struggle with his conscience, and over the objections of most close advisers, Dr. King finally moved, first against the war, accepting the criticism and loss of financial support that followed. His dissent was measured, eloquent and impressive, sending reverberations through the influential liberal circles that are still being felt.

Finding a new approach to the cities and Black Power was, however, a more complex problem, one that took more time. Dr. King's Southern Christian Leadership Conference (SCLC) was not the disciplined, efficient nonviolent cadre it sometimes seemed to be. Except for a small number of competent management people in its Atlanta headquarters handling functions, like bookkeeping, which required order and regularity, SCLC tended to operate "by the spirit," in a fashion that was by turns amusing, exasperating and even alienating to people on the outside. Anyone who dealt very often with Dr. King soon learned, for example, that he and his advisors kept their appointments by what was known as "civil rights time," a chronology only tangentially related to the schedules of most white people.

Even so, in most Southern campaigns the Conference staff was generally more efficient than its local affiliates — and its adversaries — and was able to keep effective control of situations. But when it moved north, SCLC faced political and economic organizations whose big-city slickness and sophistication left them outclassed. In the wake of the Meredith Mississippi March in June 1966 and the appearance of

Black Power as a slogan and a distinct mood, SCLC staff members began adopting more noticeably natural hair styles, wearing African dress and ornaments and appropriating substantial elements of Black Power rhetoric. Despite these adjustments, his first northern campaign, the Chicago open housing movement of 1966, ended with Dr. King being outsmarted by the city's realtors and its wily mayor, Richard J. Daley. After that Dr. King concentrated for several months on antiwar activity and writing a book. By fall of 1967, he believed time was running out, that the nation was dangerously near a race war on the one hand and a backlash-spawned rightwing takeover on the other. He felt he had to develop a program by the next summer which could produce real change for the better in black people's lives through nonviolent protest. Only such a campaign, he felt, could defuse the urban time bombs, halt the backlash, and make Vietnam too great a political and fiscal liability for an incumbent administration to carry into the presidential election. Only such a campaign, in addition, could prevent nonviolence from being further seriously discredited among black people and prevent him, as the leading advocate of nonviolence, from being discredited along with it.

This was the situation the Poor People's Campaign was conceived to meet. "Our nation," Dr. King said in his announcement of the Campaign, December 4, 1967, "is at a crossroads of history and it is critically important for us, as a nation and a society, to choose a new path and move upon it with resolution and courage.

"It is impossible to underestimate the crisis we face in America. The stability of a civilization, the potential of free government, and the simple honor of men are at stake."

Walter Rugaber, reporting for *The New York Times* on the press conference at which the announcement was made, spoke of Dr. King thus: "The Negro leader's mood seemed deeply pessimistic. He said the confrontation in Washington was a 'last desperate demand' by Negroes, an attempt to avoid 'the worst chaos, hatred and violence any nation has ever encountered.'" But, he added, Dr. King believed the "'angry and bitter' people would respond to nonviolence 'if it's militant enough, it's really doing something.'"

In his last major article, Dr. King expanded on his analysis for the readers of *Look* (April 16, 1968): "We believe that if this campaign succeeds, non-violence will again be the dominant instrument for social change — and jobs and income will be placed in the hands of the tormented poor. If it fails, non-violence will be discredited, and the country may be plunged into a holocaust — a tragedy deepened by the awareness that it was avoidable. . . .

". . . I'm convinced that if something isn't done to deal with the very harsh and real economic problems of the ghetto, the talk of guerilla warfare is going to become much more real. The nation has not yet recognized the seriousness of it. . . . As committed as I am to non-violence, I have to face this fact: if we do not get a positive response in Washington many more Negroes will begin to think and act in violent terms. . . ."

"White America has allowed itself to be indifferent to race prejudice and economic denial. It has treated them as superficial blemishes, but now awakes to the horrifying reality of a potentially fatal disease. The urban outbreaks are 'a fire bell in the night' clamorously warning that the seams of our entire social order are weakening under strains of neglect."

His language was equally ominous in his last fund-raising letter: "Our national government is playing Russian roulette with riots; it gambles with another summer of disaster. Not a single basic social cause of riots has been corrected. Though ample resources are available they are squandered substantially on war. . . . In the halls of Congress Negro lives are too cheap to justify resolute measures; it is easier to speculate in blood and do nothing.

"We intend, before the summer comes, to initiate a 'last

chance' project to arouse the American conscience toward
constructive democratic change.

"The nation has been warned by the President's Commis-
sion [on Civil Disorders] that our society faces catastrophic
division in an approaching doomsday if the country does not
act. We have, through this non-violent action, an opportunity
to avoid a national disaster and to create a new spirit of
harmony."

The overall strategic outline for the Campaign was roughly
as follows: Several thousand poor people would converge on
Washington and settle there in a highly visible shantytown.
A brief series of exploratory demonstrations would culminate
in a one-day mass rally of liberal forces. Then the Campaign
would get down to business in the form of arrest-provoking
nonviolent disruption of government operations. As the campers trooped to jail by the hundreds they were to be joined by
hundreds, even thousands more, including students from the
nation's colleges and blacks from the Washington ghetto,
whose indignation at the spectacle of poor people going to jail
for protesting their plight would be mobilized into action by
SCLC's organizers. The arrests were expected to focus widespread sympathy and attention on the marchers' cause, especially among black people around the nation. This sympathy
would be the base for the Campaign's next phase: nationwide
boycotts of selected industries and big-city shopping areas, supported by continuing demonstrations and arrests in the capital
and elsewhere. These boycotts were expected to prod business
leaders into pressuring Congress to meet the Campaign's demands, pressures the legislators would be unable to resist.

This strategy incorporated several features that had not
been part of Dr. King's previous campaigns. The boycott
plan was one. SCLC's Operation Breadbasket had for several
years run local boycotts aimed at increasing and upgrading
Negro employment. But such boycotts had never been tried
on a nationwide scale or made a central tactic of major cam-

paigns. At least once before, in early 1965, Dr. King had
directed staff members to make preparations for an all-out
nationwide boycott, in that case of products and companies
associated with Mississippi. It was to be aimed at forcing that
state to allow blacks to register and vote freely. But when the
date for announcing the boycott arrived, Dr. King backed off,
reportedly because he felt it would wreck Mississippi's economy for years to come and he was not then willing to be responsible for such an upheaval. That he was now ready to
take on the national economy indicated how grave he considered the country's plight to be.

Similarly new was his attempt to forge a coalition among
poor people of different ethnic groups, probably the most serious effort of its kind since the Depression. Dr. King traveled
thousands of miles in the early months of 1968, meeting and
negotiating with prominent Mexican-Americans, Puerto
Ricans, American Indians and poor whites. He seemed, in
those last weeks, to be making real progress towards bringing
them together under the Campaign's banner.

A third major innovation was the shift of focus implied in
the Campaign's goal of ending poverty. Dr. King's earlier
movements were based on appeals to reasonably well-defined
constitutional guarantees: the right to vote, equal protection
of the laws, freedom of assembly and petition, etc. But, as
James Bevel, one of King's best strategists, put it, "There's
nothing unconstitutional about children starving to death."
By going clearly beyond constitutional imperatives Dr. King
was demanding more than anything the liberal civil rights
movement had ever sought, except rhetorically. This meant
he could not any longer center his appeal on values all Americans were, on paper at least, committed to support. Moreover,
poverty was an issue of national dimensions, and he could
not, as in the Southern campaigns, expect sympathy in one
region to produce pressure on another.

Many external conditions, however, seemed favorable to the

Campaign. Financial experts talked uneasily about related dangers to the economy from inflation, the balance of payments, and a most unsettling war. America's black people seemed ready to do or support almost anything to make their problems visible and get action on solving them. Washington policemen were reputed to be as violent a law enforcement outfit as many in the deep South; its men could be counted on to lose their cool if given the chance and provide the Campaign with the official brutality that has always been such an effective mobilizer.

Thus, while with the Poor People's Campaign he was shooting for bigger stakes and expected to encounter much stiffer opposition than he had in his other movements, Dr. King felt that anything less would be insufficient, and he was planning to bring into play nonviolent weaponry of much larger caliber than he had used before. The groundwork for the movement was almost finished at the time of his last trip to Memphis, and Dr. King had every reason to feel that when the April 22nd kickoff day arrived, he and SCLC would be ready.

By the time the funeral was over and the city fires had subsided, the date for opening the Campaign had nearly arrived. The SCLC staff was staggering under the weight of their loss and the almost continuous labor it made necessary. But they decided to go ahead with the Campaign, now seen as the most appropriate memorial to Dr. King, as nearly according to plan as possible. Its opening salvo — a visit to Washington by King's successor, the Reverend Ralph David Abernathy, and a committee of one hundred representatives of the poor from various ethnic groups — was delayed only a week, until April 28. Shortly thereafter the first of many Campaign caravans left Memphis, headed for Washington. In the next several days other caravan parties departed from California, Maine, Washington state, Chicago, Albuquerque, the Mis-

sissippi Delta, and several other places. Busses, food and bedding were provided for them by support groups in major
cities along the way. At each stop the campaigners staged
marches and rallies to keep spirits high and gain recruits from
local areas.

This decision was to prove an unfortunate one. An event
like Dr. King's murder would have debilitated any small,
leader-oriented group; it was especially hard on SCLC because, as Action Director Hosea Williams was fond of saying,
"We are a movement, not an organization." The executive
staff apparently was gambling that, once settled in Washington, the Campaign would proceed roughly according to their
strategic scenario, and that the staff would overcome their
fatigue and grief sufficiently to carry it off.

The gamble was lost almost as soon as it had been made.
One of the major difficulties resulting from the decision to begin the Campaign as scheduled was that it permitted Ralph
Abernathy no time to establish, either in his own or in the
public's mind, a consistent and appealing leadership style and
identity as Dr. King's successor. What this lack meant was
shown early in the Campaign on May 6 when Abernathy led
the Southern Caravan into Selma, Alabama from its starting
point in Mississippi.

Selma had been the scene of what was perhaps Dr. King's
most successful campaign, when the 1965 march from there
to Montgomery moved Congress to pass a Voting Rights Act
which enfranchised hundreds of thousands of blacks across
the South. The city had not been on the original itinerary for
the Southern Caravan, and was included by Abernathy's
direct order. One felt his sense of good Baptist form would
have been offended had he not paused there to pay tribute to
and lead in mourning these people who had followed Dr.
King so loyally. A passage through the city would also be of
considerable interest to the mass media and much publicity
mileage could be wrung from it.

This writer was a junior SCLC staff member during the Selma campaign, and watched Rev. Abernathy preach in tandem with Dr. King night after night for several weeks. Abernathy usually preached last, and was noted for his earthy, penetrating exposures of the irony and silliness of segregation and segregationists. He combined reinforcement and comic relief with a down-home brilliance that was a fine complement to Dr. King's disciplined eloquence. In fact, Abernathy at his best often surpassed Dr. King in the pulpit, though without seeming to compete. He was, for instance, more original than his mentor, who had a relatively small sermon repertory. Abernathy was least effective trying to be solemn; then he was given to pomposity and embarrassing exaggeration.

When he rose to speak as the movement's new leader in Selma's Tabernacle Baptist Church, the gathered crowd was still damp-eyed from a moving blues rendition of "How Great Thou Art," played in Dr. King's memory on a battered trumpet a few moments earlier. The people remembered Abernathy as their dead leader's closest companion. That he was Dr. King's choice for a successor made sense to them as it did not to many elsewhere who had not watched them work together.

As he reached the pulpit, exhaustion showed heavy lines in his face. His voice, rasping and guttural, also reflected fatigue. Surprisingly, he spoke first of his closeness to Dr. King, as if this crowd needed to be convinced of it, taking them with him in a reflective recounting of their final hours together:

"...It became my responsibility to ride by his side, and after that to hold his hand. I stood in the operating room and refused to go out, as they performed the operation and worked untiringly to save his life. I had to go to the morgue at the Coroner's Office and identify his body. I had to arrange for the autopsy...choose his casket...choose his burial suit...

take his body from Memphis to Atlanta ... serve as the offi-
ciating minister for the largest private funeral in the history
of this country —"

The people, silent until now, responded: "That's right!
That's right!"

" — and hold together the most powerful organization in
America today, the Southern Christian Leadership Conference. I haven't had time to cry ... I haven't had time to
grieve, I haven't had time to mourn ... for my brother...."

Abernathy gripped the podium, the words trailing off.
Tears came. The crowd held its breath for a moment, then a
woman's voice broke out in an old, sorrowful chant:

"Jesus got all, all the power...."

Other voices joined her the second time:

"Lord, keep us together!" "Jesus got all, all the power."

A chorus of cries answered each phrase, and the church
wept with the man in the pulpit.

"It has been so very lonely," Abernathy said finally, in a
near whisper —

"Hmmm!"

"Since he ... went away."

"Yeah!"

"But with your help, and with God's help, we have made
up in our minds that we are going on, until victory is won."

Composure again intact, he continued, admonishing the
people to stick together behind their leadership and recalling
what had been accomplished in Selma. Then, referring to the
press as one tool of those who would divide black people, he
suddenly shifted away from Selma into a tirade against press
criticism of his lateness for several appointments with Cabinet
members the previous week. No one in the audience but the
reporters clustered around the dais understood what he was
referring to; but the people whooped and applauded obediently as he excoriated his critics:

"The press said I came to town *late* and gave no explanation. Number one, don't no white man pay *my* salary, why must I explain why I'm late? I am only accountable to the West Hunter St. Baptist Church that pays my salary and to the black people of this movement! These are the only people that I am accountable to....

"They said Ralph Abernathy was late. But you know, I lived with Martin Luther King. *Nobody* loved him as much as I do — nobody, I don't care who he is: Marty, Yogi, Dexter, Mrs. King or any of 'em. Nobody loved him more than I do. And nobody knew as much about him. I knew his thoughts. I knew his mind. I knew his innermost secrets — and I ain't gon' tell *you* what they were. [Laughter.] But let me make it plain: in spite of my love for him, tell me: when did Martin Luther King get *any*where on time? In spite of my love for him, when did *he* make a press conference on time?"

Abernathy was not finished. "And now they want to set up some kind of comparison between me and Martin Luther King. Number one, I am *Ralph David Abernathy*. I've been Ralph David Abernathy for 42 years. And every time I look in the mirror in the morning I look better and better. [Laughter and cheers.] I have three little children, two girls and a boy, and every day they tell me that I'm the sweetest daddy in the world, and they wouldn't swap me for Lyndon Baines Johnson. [Laughter.] I have a *wife*. She's black — but Lord knows she's beautiful. [Wild applause.] You know her, she doesn't even have a pimple on her face, ain't had a bump on her face in the past twenty years. Smooth and beautiful, smiling and wonderful, she tells me every night that my kisses are sweeter than wine. [Wild laughter and applause.] So you may as well do justice one to the other, because if you're trying to make Martin Luther King outa me, I got news for you. I love Ralph Abernathy as he is too good to give up Ralph Abernathy to be *any*body. I'm gonna be nobody *but*

Ralph Abernathy, and Lord knows with me you gonna have
hell on your hands...! [Laughter and applause.]

"God has put every man out to do a special job, and to do
a special task. And I make no apologies for what I can do.
Number one, I'm a natural-*born* leader." ["You're right!"]
Before sperm met spermatazo, before I was conceived in my,
in my mother's womb, way back yonder before time started
groping, God ordained that I would *lead* men. Why, if I walk
outa this church right now, everybody in here will walk out
behind me...."

"One day the press said to me, 'Rev. Abernathy, usually the
press always gives a man a honeymoon period; but they
didn't ever give you a honeymoon.' I said, well that's all right,
I don't speak for the press. I'm not concerned about the press,
I'm concerned about my people. All I want to do is to get
my *black* people together, and to get my Mexican-Americans,
and my American Indians, and my Puerto Ricans and get all
of them together; that's all — and the poor white people in
the Appalachian areas, that's all I want to do is get them together. And then I'm going to hire eight or ten secretaries to
make arrangements for the press that's going to be knocking
at *my* door wanting an interview. [Laughter and applause.]

"You know how to deal with the press? The way you deal
with the press — you don't deal with the press by sending out
press releases and all o' that, what you do is get somethin'
goin' and then these men here are paid for a story; if they
don't get a story, they gonna be fired. [Laughter.] So don't
get it in your mind that CBS, NBC, ABC, or any *other*
kinda C [laughter], has sent them out here for their health.
They have sent them out here for a story. And all you've got
to do is to produce the story. And I have made up in my
mind, with the help of God, I am *going* to produce that
story." [Applause.]

He spoke of the progress of the Campaign so far and its
determination "to stay in Washington until Congress decided

to do something about our plight," but interrupted himself again to demand a retraction from a Washington newspaper (he couldn't recall the name) which, he charged, reported falsely that he had called someone a honky.

The performance surprised and disappointed the newsmen and this writer. We had heard almost nothing from the Abernathy of three years before; now, except for the very real pathos of his tribute to Dr. King, there was little but the bombast and crowd-pleasing exaggeration that had marred only a few of his many fine earlier sermons. He was not often thereafter so thin-skinned and snappish, but his preaching throughout the rest of the summer never became very impressive.

In view of his capacity for real eloquence, however, as well as the importance of his contribution to Dr. King's success, the conclusion reached by many observers from his public appearances, that Abernathy was a nonentity whose elevation to King's position was a mistake, does not carry much weight. The contention rests on an uncritical acceptance of Dr. King's stature, an acceptance that does not look at its base, the pedestal on which King was elevated. One of Dr. King's former advisors put it best: "Ralph's biggest problem was that Martin was dead. But if *Ralph* had been killed, Martin would have been equally at sea. That's how important their relationship was."

Dr. King's eminence was not entirely the result of his courage and skill at leading nonviolent movements. It was also to a considerable extent the product of a careful, methodical process of image-building over more than a decade; and Ralph Abernathy was a key man in this process. Hosea Williams described their interdependence in the *New York Times Sunday Magazine*: "Ralph was the unsung hero of the civil rights movement. Martin wouldn't make a decision without him. He trusted Ralph like he

trusted Jesus. Ralph gave him confidence, security, a strong
soul to lean on. On the other hand, he gave Ralph his brilliance, his eloquence and intellectual depth, that charisma
the white press is always talking about."* Abernathy himself
hinted at the extent of his role in an aside during the Selma
speech: "I wanta say this — I don't wanta have to say it ["Say
it!"], but I just got to say it anyhow ["Say it!"]. I shouldn't
have to say it ["Say it!"], but I just have to say it ["Say it!"
and laughter]. Because you see, when there was a Dr. King
there was always a Ralph Abernathy to say it. But there isn't
— I don't have a Ralph Abernathy like Dr. King; you see I
took care of certain things so he didn't have to say certain
things. Now that's why he could get up and talk philosophy,
because I had taken care of some other things. You all understand that? So since — since I don't have a Ralph Abernathy,
I'll have to say it myself: I been listening on the radio all this
afternoon, 'The Poor People's Campaign got started outa
Mississippi today' — talking like its a leaderless campaign.
The Poor People's Campaign has a leader, a darn good leader,
by the name of Ralph David Abernathy. [Cheers.]"

This suggests some of the ways Abernathy helped sustain
Dr. King's position. When the primacy of King's leadership
needed emphasizing before a particular group, it was Abernathy who emphasized it so King did not need to talk ego-
tistically about himself. If a crowd was hostile, it was Abernathy who spoke first, absorbing and disarming the antagon-
ism so Dr. King could "talk philosophy" unchallenged. Even
within SCLC, according to reliable information, Dr. King
disliked becoming involved in any agitation; he would often,
after listening carefully to both sides of a dispute between
staff members, turn to his friend and say, "Ralph, you take
care of it"; and Ralph always did. When Dr. King went to
jail, Ralph almost always went with him. They worked out a

* " 'No Man Can Fill Dr. King's Shoes' — But Abernathy Tries," by
Paul Good, N. Y. Times Magazine, May 26, 1968.

definite regimen of exercise, fasting, meditation, and prayer which they followed together to pass and make profitable their days in prison.

Perhaps not until historians begin trying to understand and trace Dr. King's rise will the extent and importance of Ralph Abernathy's contribution be appreciated; it can only be suggested here. But having operated for so long as one-half of a team, he was not, as the Southern Caravan proceeded through Alabama, yet able to project both halves of this team successfully through one personality. "I had thought they would kill us together," he told writer Paul Good, in the *Times* magazine article quoted above, on the trip to Selma. "I never thought the day would come I'd have to live without Martin. But he always told me they would get him first." The decision to press forward with the Campaign despite Abernathy's fatigue and uncertainty left him no time in the ensuing turbulent weeks to do the thinking, praying, and experimenting needed to develop an effective personal style that made the best of his considerable abilities.

Abernathy's uncertain performance was a factor in a post-assassination decline of SCLC in the eyes of the white liberals who had thought so highly of Dr. King. A few days after leaving Selma, for instance, he spoke at a Boston fund-raising luncheon attended by such brahmins as ex-governor and Mrs. Thomas Peabody. The Peabodys were old patrons of the movement; the governor's mother had even gone to jail in St. Augustine, Florida, for Dr. King in 1964. But Abernathy, who arrived late, whose speech was dull and whose jokes seemed crude, left the patrician audience cool and unamused. His effect on most white audiences through the summer, both live and in the media, was much the same.

A basic restructuring of the relationship between SCLC and its white liberal constituency was probably inevitable upon Abernathy's elevation in any case, because he was such a different kind of person than his predecessor. Dr. King was an aristocrat, raised in the upper levels of Atlanta's black professional class and educated at Morehouse, an elite black college. His PhD from northern, white Boston University guaranteed status among Negro preachers and provided entree with white intellectuals. As he rose to prominence, his temperament and accomplishments fitted him admirably into the white liberal elite represented by the Peabodys, the National Council of Churches, and the *New York Times*. He seemed, in fact, more at home preaching in Manhattan's wealthy Riverside Church than in the shabby Negro tabernacles in which his movements were head-quartered. And as his leadership image was constructed, its effect on this white elite was given as much and often more consideration than its effect on the black masses.

Ralph Abernathy, on the other hand, grew up on a farm in isolated, black-belt Marengo County, Alabama. Three years ago he brought down the house in Selma churches with the story of his first goggle-eyed and breathless boyhood visits to their metropolis, which must have been all of 15,000 population then but was the largest city he had ever seen. His alma mater was Alabama State in Montgomery, a pathetic, unaccredited state institution that was not much more than a self-debunking sop to Alabama's separate-but-equal mythology. Completed with a master's at Atlanta University, his education left him a solid member of the black urban middle class, but his rural roots were never com-pletely left behind, remaining noticeable as we have seen in his speaking style. Where Dr. King went over the heads of rapt but semi-literate black audiences with occasional refer-ences to the *zeitgeist* and *agape*, Ralph socked the same points to them with such stories as how the Birmingham movement turned Bull Connor into a steer.

Such a story would sound rather out of place at the River-side Church, and did sound out of place when Abernathy told it to his Boston audience. If nothing else, Abernathy's personality thus made it almost certain that he would not have the same rapport with white liberals Dr. King had enjoyed. There seems to be no reason, however, why given time they could not learn to respect him as a capable leader with skills and accomplishments of his own. But as the Campaign developed he had no time even to define a position of his own. He continued to look and sound like only a blurred and less-refined echo of his Atlanta mentor.

Still, the Campaign's prospects appeared good as the Southern Caravan marched across Selma's Edmund Pettus Bridge the afternoon of May 7 to mark the spot where 600 Black citizens had been attacked by state troopers and by mounted sheriff's deputies in March 1965. Press coverage, though not all friendly, was heavy. The wave of white sympathy and guilt that followed Dr. King's murder was still pouring contributions into SCLC's treasury. Crowds at nightly rallies along the several caravan routes were large, enthusiastic, and hospitable. And the Campaign's Washington staff was confident of finding a suitable site for the building of the Campaign's shantytown, probably in government parkland not far from the Lincoln Memorial.

2

City of Hope

Watching the approach of the Poor People's several caravans, the heavily Southern-oriented white Washington region felt surrounded, with dynamite at its center and fuses sputtering towards it from all directions. Along 7th and 14th Streets, N. W., block after block of blasted stores and burntout apartments stood like displays of junk sculpture, and the uprising that produced them was still imprinted on everyone's memory. In early May a series of nighttime bus robberies by blacks, culminating in the murder of a driver, resulted in a disruptive wildcat transit strike; these events were given heavy play in the local media, helping to keep whites on the edge of panic. Some Congressmen were telling constituents it was not safe to visit the capital, and tourists, the city's second largest source of revenue, were already staying away in droves. Employers in the District reportedly were having difficulty finding workers, especially for night shifts. Radio talkback shows and letters-to-the-editor columns were filled with high-pitched calls for law and order, the lifting of restrictions on police activity, and the shooting of looters. Local editors and columnists shared this uneasiness. Taking up a suggestion first made by Illinois Senator Charles Percy, *The Washington Post* in an editorial on April 23 tried to discourage the leaders without sounding illiberal: "Would more Americans better understand the plight of the rural and urban poor if, through the eyes of their press and their governmental spokesmen, they visited the poison spots of poverty, instead of bringing representatives of these regions into the Capitol?...Let us have a march, by all means. But why not turn it around and have its route run from Washington to where the poverty is, instead of from where the poverty is to Washington?"

Columist Richard Wilson, writing in the *Evening Star* on May 1, was more direct: "The march was poorly conceived from the beginning. Its objectives are not clearly spelled out. Its potential for harm is probably greater than for good. But it is not possible to convince its leaders of this.... What is most discouraging about all this is that need does exist, inequalities want correction, but the methods chosen to dramatize the needs are likely to have the opposite effect." But the *Star's* editors, once it was clear the march could not be prevented, were grimly philosophical about it: "The Poor People's Campaign might help to advance these [antipoverty] developments — or it could set them back disastrously," they wrote on May 12. "That is the issue truly at stake in the days and weeks immediately ahead."

These reactions were not all paranoid fantasy. The District of Columbia's finances are still controlled by Southern-dominated Congressional Committees, and public services, especially schools and welfare facilities, are in a wretched state that has helped to drive whites into segregated Virginia and Maryland suburbs. As blacks continue migrating to the city from the South, the inadequacies of these institutions assist the formation of the "urban proletariat" that provides the fuel for most uprisings. The main reason, it is believed, why there were no earlier revolts in the District is that so many of its black citizens either have comparatively comfortable government jobs or are supported by others who do. Until the spring of 1968, the most alienated people had tended to settle for crime, alcohol, and drugs as outlets. The ghetto had never really been calm; but now, after the April explosion, everyone finally understood that its present quietude could not be seen as tranquility.

Into this situation the poor people, mostly black, were coming, in Abernathy's words, to "turn things upside down and right side up." Southern Senators competed in denouncing the Campaign. Senator McClellan of Arkansas called it "a premeditated act of contempt for and rebellion against the sovereignty of government," and announced he had "sworn information" of a militant plot to turn the Campaign to violence. Senator Jennings Randolph of West Virginia detected "strong evidence of Communist planning and participation." Senator Russell Long of Louisiana won the prize with his vow to demand censure or expulsion of any Senator who advocated "bending the knee" to the demonstrators. "When that bunch of marchers comes here," he raged, "they can just burn the whole place down and we can move the capital to some place where they enforce the law." He was especially upset by talk of a guaranteed income: "If they think they are going to push us into bankrupting this country to pay worthless people to be more worthless, they are making a mistake." Several bills were introduced to prohibit construction of a shantytown on any government parkland.

The Campaign staff in Washington, including National Co-ordinator Rev. Bernard Lafayette, kept up the suspense by touring the Mall to look over likely campsites and at the same time expressing no interest in applying for a permit to use the land they decided on. Concurrently, however, behind-the-scenes negotiations went on for nearly a week between Campaign spokesmen, federal and District officials. Agreement on the terms of a permit was never seriously in doubt, and a permit was issued on May 10 by the National Park Service. The permit, for use of 15 acres of West Potomac Park between the Reflecting Pool and Independence Avenue, from the Lincoln Memorial to 17th Street, limited the shantytown's population to 3,000. It was good until June 16, but allowed for extensions at the government's discretion. SCLC was required to post a $5,000 bond to cover possible damages. The government attempted to mollify anti-march sentiment in Congress and fear in the suburbs by letting it be known when the permit was granted that 8,000 federal troops, many of them Vietnam veterans, along with 1,800 D.C. National Guardsmen, were being alerted for possible duty, and that the Defense Department had ready a detailed plan for their deployment in the event violence occurred.

Despite the predominant white feeling of near hysteria as the caravans closed in on the capital, there were sizeable support efforts being organized among sympathetic area residents to provide the campaigners with food, temporary shelter, clothing, and medical care. When the first two busloads arrived from Atlanta early Saturday, May 11, they were greeted at an Arlington Catholic church by a crowd of mostly white volunteers that easily outnumbered them. Local businessmen and churches formed an Ad Hoc Committee to work with the Washington Urban Coalition in providing food for the campaigners. Hundreds were calling and visiting SCLC Headquarters at 14th and U Streets, N.W., to sign up for volunteer work. On Sunday the 12th, 6,000 people attended a Mother's Day rally at the Cardoza High School stadium which was addressed by Mrs. Martin Luther King and sponsored by the National Welfare Rights Organization in conjunction with the campaign. The 450 members of the Mid-South Caravan, dubbed the Memphis Freedom Train, which had left from Memphis and traveled across Tennessee and up through Virginia, arrived Sunday afternoon to find ample accommodations awaiting them in District churches until the shantytown, now named Resurrection City, was ready to house them, which the staff expected to be no later than the following night.

Rev. Abernathy was scheduled to drive the first stake in the construction of Resurrection City at 10:00 A.M. Monday morning, May 13. But of course he was late; and the crowd of well-wishers, reporters, and cameramen that was there on time amused itself by fiddling with equipment or strolling around on the cool grass. A double column of about 50 marchers from the Mid-South Caravan appeared a few minutes later, walking around the southwest corner of the reflecting pool toward the piles of prefabricated plywood wall sections lying a hundred yards or so away. Reporters and photographers immediately surrounded the group, shutters snapping, microphones extended. And just as quickly, young men who called themselves marshals began barking orders, first to the marchers not to talk to the press, and then at the press to go away and stop taking pictures. The photographers were a little surprised, but shrugged it off and went on shooting; reporters likewise paused, then moved back in. But the marshals were insistent and hostile, intercepting and squelching any attempted interviews, stepping between the photographers and their subjects.

There were no explanations, and once it was clear that neither Abernathy nor any of his top staff was with the group, the newsmen retreated, turning back to the spot where the opening ceremony was to be conducted. There they went about their business, stretching cables back and forth, jockeying for shooting positions and getting settled in a tight semicircle around a gray bouquet of microphones. The marchers soon evaded their marshals and gathered outside this circle waiting for the action to start, but they were too intimidated now to answer any questions. One by one the marshals joined them, and several began ordering reporters to move back so they could see better. The cameramen, now irritated, studiously paid no attention. When the marshals persisted and raised their voices, arguments broke out. One marshal got so upset two others appeared at his side to restrain him. The situation quickly became a standoff, with angry reporters crouching or sitting on the grass but keeping their places while marshals and marchers kept up constant but less insistent cries for them to move.

The tension eased when a man calling himself an SCLC press co-ordinator arrived, assured everyone that their leader would be along shortly, and introduced the Hill family, which had been chosen to occupy the first shanty. Mrs. Minnie Lee Hill was from Marks, Mississippi, where her husband earned $155 a month working for the city. Mrs. Hill was the mother of 17 children, 12 of whom were living and 8 of whom were with her. The press co-ordinator supplied this information as Mrs. Hill, like the rest of her group, had been told not to speak with the press.

Abernathy finally showed up, not quite two hours behind schedule. Wearing a Levi jacket, no shirt and a carpenter's apron, still looking exhausted, he thanked Rev. Bernard Lafayette for his introduction, led the crowd in "We Shall Overcome," and quoted a passage from Scripture that now sounds ironic:

"Except the Lord build the house, then they labor in vain who build it.

"Fret not thyself because of evildoers.... Trust in the Lord and do good. So shall thou dwell in the land, and verily thou shalt be fed.... Fret not thyself in any wise to do evil, for evildoers shall be cut off. But those that wait upon the Lord, they shall inherit the earth."

Abernathy reiterated the Campaign's intention to stay in Washington "not just for a *day*." But as he raised his voice to emphasize "or even a *week* — " he was drowned out by a jet airliner passing overhead on final approach to National Airport. He paused, pique showing in the fatigue lines; he did not like being interrupted. The noise faded away and Abernathy went on: "We will be here in Washington until the Congress of the United States and the leaders of the

various departments of our government decide that they are
going to do something about the plight of poor people in this
country by doing away with poverty, unemployment, and
underemployment in this country.

"We're going to build this city... and here we will build a
Koinonia, a community of love and brotherhood. American
Indians, Puerto Ricans, Mexican-Americans, white poor
Americans from the Appalachian area of our country and
black Americans will all live together here in this city of
hope. It may be that we will have some squabbles among
ourselves. But I want to set the record straight for you now:
that if we have any squabbles, they are going to all be in the
family and we are going to solve these squabbles among ourselves."

He continued, pledging to be nonviolent but militant, scattering platitudes in every direction. Airliners interrupted him
twice more. Then, moving back to the spot designated for the
first shanty, he posed with a hammer upheld and drove a nail
into a stake, the crowd chanting "Freedom! Freedom! Freedom!" in time with the blows. Several volunteers moved in
with the shanty's frame and walls; after driving a few more
nails, Abernathy gave up the hammer and apron, shook
hands on the way to his car, and was gone to a press conference at the Pitts Motel, a black-owned, well-appointed establishment where he and most of the professional staff had
rooms.

Fifty of the shanties, tentlike A-frame structures of plywood
and sheet plastic, were completed by nightfall. Digging and
wiring for electric power and sewage had also begun but
moved slowly. The first 300 residents moved in the following day, spending Tuesday night shivering around open
campfires in the cold spring air.

By Tuesday afternoon a snow fence had been thrown up
around the shanties, its few gates jealously guarded by the

marshals. These were a shifting group of largely self-selected black men, many from slum gangs. Most seemed to enjoy their new authority and many used it to express hostility for sightseers in general, whites in particular, and newsmen especially — all of whom clustered around this newest public attraction. Encounters like those of the first morning between guards and reporters became constant occurrences; but now with the snow fence up, the marshals were able to keep reporters well away from their subjects.

The marshals' attitude came as a sharp surprise to the reporters covering the camp. It was not at all like SCLC to treat them this way; before, Dr. King and his staff had always worked hard to keep the press on their side. Many if not most of the newsmen assigned to the site considered themselves sympathetic to the undertaking, and it was a shock and an affront to have their attentions spurned. A reaction was not long in coming: in Tuesday's *Evening Star* the highly regarded columnist Mary McGrory detailed some of the rebuffs under the headline "Oppressed are Oppressing." "The young marshals," she wrote, "some of whom probably have shouted themselves hoarse over police brutality, were pushing people around in the style to which they have become accustomed. Their orders were numerous and arbitrary. They shouted 'make way,' joined hands, shoved organizers, sympathizers and curious indiscriminately, intervened swiftly in any dialogue between poor and press."

It was not an unfair description, and as this feedback filtered up the chain of command, SCLC became concerned but was uncertain what to do about it. On the one hand, press sympathy was vitally important to the Campaign; but on the other, the group from which most marshals came — loosely and not too accurately dubbed "militants" — was the group whose loyalty to nonviolence SCLC was least certain of. Their allegiance was being vigorously competed for by nationalist and separatist groups, and many of them in the

camp had only taken the pledge of nonviolence for the summer in deference to Dr. King's memory. If the leadership
were now to rebuke them in favor of the "honky" press, these
"militants" could not be counted on to stay in the Campaign,
and might even take their frustrations into Washington's
smoldering ghetto.

The SCLC staff members found themselves in a quandary.
While they vacillated, spokesmen at the site tried to play
both ends against the middle, making exceptions to the
marshals' rules and keeping the reporters mystified with long
philosophical spiels about how everything was actually under
control and going according to the higher logic of nonviolent
theory, hoping all the while that by tomorrow or the next
day the marshals would calm down and leave the newsmen
alone. "This is a community of brotherhood," James Bevel
explained at one point; "we are all learning from each other
— everybody is a student and everybody is sacred. Because we
operate on a brotherhood concept and not on authoritarian
thinking, the police and the press get frustrated. I'm not intimidated by a loose, unstructured group of people." Bevel
and the other top staff appeared several times daily outside
the fence, assuring reporters they had free access to the
city and occasionally leading a brief tour of the site past the
disgruntled marshals. "We have no fronts and no games,"
he told them at one point. "You can talk to the people and
find out why they're here. But give people in this camp the
same respect you'd give to Luci, Lynda, and Lady Bird." As
soon as Bevel faded into the crowd, which he usually did
after a few minutes, marshals closed in to throw the reporters
out and taunt them again from the gates.

This juggling reached a peak on Wednesday night, May
15. A town meeting was scheduled for 8:00 P.M., and the
announced agenda included the setting up of a government
for Resurrection City — and discussion of the role of the press.

At first reporters were told they could attend the meeting. Then they were told they couldn't. Bevel, who was sought out to clarify the matter, again told them they would be admitted, but confined to one section, and might be asked to leave if some residents wanted to discuss "personal matters." When the cameramen and soundmen arrived at the gate about 7:45, loaded with equipment, they were once more refused entry and stood around cursing until a white SCLC press aide met them and said he was trying to find Bevel. Bevel arrived, let them through the gate, and disappeared. This got the newsmen as far as the meeting tent, where marshals again barred the entrance until Bevel returned to clear the way.

Once inside, the reporters set up quietly and without further interference. The residents drifted in, and the Rev. F. D. Kirkpatrick, a big, serious-looking man who had once been an official of Louisiana's Deacons for Defense, led them with a deep, powerful voice through a long and enthusiastic series of freedom songs. Throughout the songfest, Bevel, Lafayette, and other high-level staff held a whispered conference in a corner.

About 9:30 the singing subsided and speeches began. The Rev. Bernard Lafayette was first. He summarized Campaign developments and offhandedly informed the audience that the camp's government would *not* be set up that night after all. He introduced Lance "Sweet Willie" Washington, leader of the Invaders, a gang from Memphis that had disrupted Dr. King's early Memphis marches but now had joined the Campaign. Sweet Willie wore beads, shades, and one dangling earring, and he talked soulfully of how the Campaign was going to, in the words of a current dance, "tighten up" Washington. "Looka here: what we gon' do, we gon' form ourselves into a big ol' *wrench,* and we gonna do a little 'tighten up.' ["Yeah!" cried the people] ... We gonna get together, we gonna get this big ol' wrench and put it right around Johnson's neck, we gon' [he let them say it: *"Tighten*

up!" Shouts of *"Yeah!"* and *"Soul Power!"*]. You know what
we gon' do then? After we see Johnson, we goin' to the John-
sonettes — that's Congress — we gon' ["Tighten up!"]. We
gon' leave there, we goin' straight to Lady Bird, we gonna
["Tighten up!"]. We goin' right on to Lucy Bird ["Tighten
up!"], right on to Lynda Bird ["Tighten up!"]; I hear some
o' these little black babies fixin' to go get Tweetie Bird [cheers
and laughter] . . . ! Now we didn't come up here to play.
["No!"] And I ain't throwin' no gasoline, cause that ain't
nothin'. ["No!"] They ask us, "Did ya'll come here to burn?"
Now we didn't come here to burn ["No!"], we come to make
ya'll *learn* *["Yeah!"]*, that's what we come up here to do!"

Next came Albert Sampson, a short, modishly dressed
SCLC worker from North Carolina. Sampson fancied himself a great orator, and was probably under orders to let out
the stops. He preached for an hour, and it was clear after a
few minutes that he was just killing time, piling pseudo-
literary allusions onto lines from old spirituals, and throwing
in an extended imaginary conversation in heaven between
Dr. King's spirit and Truth, Illusion, Misconception as well
as numerous other celestial abstractions. Sampson was pro-
ficient at maneuvering his rhetorical vehicle, and many in
his audience, including many reporters, never seemed to de-
tect that it was going around in circles. Those who did, however, were quite bored by the time he finished.

Bevel took the microphone last, speaking more slowly and
more interestingly about the uselessness of violence and the
kind of community he saw developing in Resurrection City.
He said they would develop among themselves "natural"
rather than "unnatural" leaders. "Let me explain to you what
we call 'natural leaders' and 'unnatural leaders'; Mayor Daley
of Chicago is an unnatural leader, because he has to steal,
murder people, *buy* the Mafia, *buy* votes, scare folks, and
threaten to cut off their food in order to make people follow
him. Malcolm X was a natural leader. He was not elected —

but folks followed him 'cause he was goin' someplace. Martin
Luther King was *another* natural leader. People followed him
because he was goin' someplace. But Johnson is *not* a natural
leader, he has to militarily intimidate folks, lest they go away
from him. . . .

"We will not *have* the kind of *sick* competitive *elections*
like white folks, where you pit brothers against brothers and
buyin' votes and schemin' and callin' that *democracy*. Democracy's based on intelligence and self-respect and respect
for other people. *What* we will *do,* we will let intelligence
lead us. When you see a man acting intelligent an' gettin'
things *done,* then you don't have to *vote* for him, its under-
stood that he's a leader. See what I mean? Like, you know, I
see some guys marry women and they goin' about 10 miles
an hour, the wife's goin' 50 an' they want the wife to walk
behind *them.* [Laughter.] They ain't even goin' no place.
See? That's what's wrong with white America: they got all
them intelligent women locked up in the suburbs, drivin'
station wagons aroun' and changin' diapers, with a bunch
o' sick ol' ignorant men over in Congress with nothin' on
their minds and they ain't goin' nowhere."

The process of selecting natural leaders was to begin in
workshops the next day, and "because we have to get our
work done while we are in our groups, working to get ourselves organized so we can move ahead, we gonna ask you
[the press] to not come in and bother us at that period."
Showers would be installed tomorrow, he promised, and before long the city would even have its own radio station.
The station was to be constructed by young people in the
camp, who would also, he said, build their own receivers.
Then he led the group in "We Shall Overcome," and the
meeting was over.

A surprising aspect of this gathering was that few if any
of the newsmen who had worked so hard to get in perceived
that the staff had finessed everyone by turning it into a re-

vival session and skillfully precluding any discussion of the
matters the meeting was ostensibly about. Everyone was temporarily mollified: the press because it was there, and the
"militants" because the reporters had seen nothing of substance, and were to be excluded from the next day's more
serious workshops. Many reporters probably did not care what
went on as long as they had their copy, tapes, and films. But
especially in their questioning of the leaders at press con-
ferences during that week and later in the Campaign, most
Washington newsmen continued to exhibit little capacity to
see through any but the most obvious of the pious nonsense
that was being spread right and left around West Potomac
Park.

It is thus surprising that SCLC was unable to manage
the press better than it did. By Friday, May 17, most newsmen were getting fed up with the petty harassment they
continued to encounter from the marshals and with the
now obvious runaround by staff at the camp, and their sym-
pathies with the Campaign were rapidly cooling. Editorial
desks in the capital had never liked the march in the first
place, and a press conference Friday afternoon virtually guaranteed that the disgusted reporters would begin feeding them
the kind of copy they wanted.

The press conference was called by Rev. Bernard Lafayette,
the National Coordinator, for one o'clock at the historic New
York Avenue Presbyterian Church three blocks from the
White House. By that hour the conference room was filled
with reporters anxious to begin asking questions. Campaign
spokesmen had for most of the week expressed confidence
that the city's 600 units would be completed by the weekend.
But with the weekend now at hand, barely a third of the
shanties were ready and construction had been practically
halted by frequent thunderstorms and what seemed to be a
sudden shortage of money and materials. No showers had

been installed and electricity was still scarce. About 500 campaigners were living at the site; 350 more were crowded into several District churches. The Northeast Caravan, said to be 800 strong, was arriving that afternoon in suburban Greenbelt, Maryland; on Saturday the Midwest and Southern Caravans with about 1,700 more were also scheduled to reach the area.

These hundreds were far more than could be housed even temporarily in available area churches; and already local white pastors, confronting flesh and blood poor people crowded restlessly and untidily into their expensive church facilities, were becoming alarmed at the prospect of having to deal with more. The situation had become serious enough by Thursday to force march leaders into a marathon meeting in the District Building with Mayor Walter Washington, federal officials, business and church leaders. The churchmen reportedly told the Campaign heads they were unwilling to house anymore campaigners and wanted those now in their churches to be out by the next day, Saturday, May 18.

Rev. Lafayette was expected to give some details about the building slowdown and the Campaign's plans for accommodating the incoming caravans. When he had not appeared by 1:30, no one was surprised. The church's noted pastor, Rev. George Docherty, dropped in a few minutes later and drew a chuckle with an offer to preach a sermon until the conference got started. But by 2:15 the newsmen were getting restive. Tom Offenburger, a Campaign press officer, hesitantly approached the microphones to assure the audience Lafayette would be there at "2:30 sharp" and to pass ten minutes reading Rev. Abernathy's schedule, the present locations and sizes of the various caravans, and indicating he didn't know the answers to their questions.

At twenty to three the reporters had had enough. Several stood up, dismantled their equipment and moved toward the door. Within a few seconds everyone was up, heading for the hall. Just as they entered the hallway Lafayette appeared, walking rapidly in their direction. After some confusion everyone returned, the microphones were replaced and Lafayette, with a brief apology, began.

"We are in the midst of the nation's most dramatic campaign — civil rights activity — not just of the twentieth century, but perhaps of all time. Never before has this nation been so moved to take social action to resolve economic problems. . . .

"We want to emphasize today, and announce, another date, which will perhaps be the largest number of people participating in a demonstration in one day in the history of America. That day is a holiday, May 30th. We are expecting no less than a million people to arrive in Washington on May 30th to participate in the nation's largest demonstration."

He asked supporters of the movement who were not presently enroute with the caravans to postpone coming to Washington until May 30.

"The other thing we'd like to say is that we are in a financial crisis at this time." The overwhelming response to the Campaign, he explained, had involved unanticipated travel expenses that were depleting SCLC's construction funds.

The questions began. Were they having fund-raising problems? How could they finance demonstrations if they didn't have enough money to finish Resurrection City?

"When we decided to go into this Campaign last year," Lafayette replied, "we were in a deficit at that time. . . . But we decided that this Campaign was so important and so necessary for the health and the growth and progress of our nation that, although the normal channel is to have a budget already outlined and the funds et cetera on hand . . . we couldn't wait until we would have accumulated the amount of money necessary for this Campaign. So in Dr. King's own words, he said he would put the organization and himself on line and go broke if necessary, but this Campaign had to go through. The whole nation and this country needs a non-violent, positive, aggressive Campaign in order to save the nation. So we have acted on faith...faith in the American people who have given overwhelming support, in the Northern areas and even Southern whites.... So although we are now in the dawn of the Campaign, we feel by noon — when the sun is shining bright — that the American people will come through...."

How much did they need?

"It's very difficult to put a total figure on it, but immediately 3 million dollars would certainly help us complete and provide the housing for all the additional people that have come in, plus it would help us complete our original planned structures."

Was the 3 million in addition to the contributions already received?

"The 3 million we're talking about is the amount of money it would take to complete the physical structures, the buildings, on the site. This figure is based on the actual expenses for the purchase of material and the construction of those units."

Three million on *construction?*

"When we talk about the 3 million dollars, we're talking about for the facility itself. This does not include the incidental expenses of the individuals, it does not include transportation, it does not include food which is certainly a costly item, and some of the food has been donated but a good deal of the food has to be bought.... And this does not include other additional expenses such as the extra tent that we had to put up, the one that you were in the other night...it does not include the carpenter's tools and that sort of thing. This is sort of a round-off figure, and as we say we can't go into too much detail about the details of this thing; this is an over-all estimate according to, you know, the people who are actually doing the purchasing and involved in finance."

"Mr. Lafayette, a couple days ago your architect estimated that the per unit cost of one of these cabins was $80. Now if you have 600 units that would come to $48,000, which means that you're saying you need $2,952,000 for everything else?"

"That's right."

"Mr. Lafayette, I think there's a very serious point here —"

"Uh, just one other question."

"The impression that you gave by that last figure is that the shelters cost $48,000 but that for installations of various kinds it's going to cost over 2 million dollars. A lot of people are going to ask the question —"

"Uh, let me say this —"

"This money, where's it going? I think you should clarify this in your own interest."

"Uh, I think we should clarify this. I'm not prepared to be interrogated on the details of this. We did say an overall round-off figure, and this was given to us by those who are, you know, doing this. Now if the press want to do this, then it's up to them. We can't help that. I think if you want to give the public a false impression, we have no control over that. You have that —"

Pandemonium. Then a senior correspondent from NBC stood up in the back, his voice and status quieting the rest: "Mr. Lafayette, let me explain something on behalf of the people here. We were invited here to meet with you at one this afternoon. You arrived at about eight minutes to three. Now there's a lot of folks here who have a lot of other things to do. We would like to cover your Campaign as fully as we possibly can, and we intend to. But you arrived just at the last possible moment, because most of these ladies and gentlemen were in the process of leaving the room. Now this doesn't mean that everything has to start within three seconds of when you say you're going to hold your conference. But you're creating a very bad impression here among the reporters here, and that's just for *openers*. For you to come in with a figure of 3 million dollars without any substantiation is kind of ridiculous, if you want us to be your agents as you say you have, you say you want the press to get the word out to the public. The press doesn't know what to do, the press can't take a figure like that and tell the public what it is unless you tell us.

"I would hope that in the future when you are going to hold a news conference and you are speaking for the whole Poor People's Campaign that you would: number one, conduct it on time, and number two, please have the figures or the information at your fingertips; because these people, they're just not going to stand for it."

"I won't give you a reason," LaFayette answered, "because I know it would only satisfy me —"

"We don't need any reasons," said the reporter.

"— Uh, may I finish please? — You did make the point that we were late. And of course there are reasons; we won't go into those. We accept the criticism, and we apologize for the tardiness. We will do our utmost best to avoid this sort of thing in the future, and on the question of the breakdown we accept that suggestion of being more specific and we're very grateful to you for makin' that observation."

"Can you tell us now," another newsman asked, "what some of that breakdown is?"

"We said that we will not deal with that now, but we will accept that suggestion and try to do that at our next news conference." A number of people tried to ask questions, but he brushed them off. "Excuse me, I'm sorry, I really must leave, I'm sorry, I'm sorry, we can't go any further — because," he was raising his voice, "if I stay here any longer I'll be late for another *meet*ing." They laughted cynically as he headed for the door.

Saturday's papers printed the story just as they heard it: one million people and 3 million dollars, adding that no breakdown was given. The Rev. Andrew Young, SCLC

Executive Vice-President, "clarified" the figures on his return
from a fund-raising trip to the west coast. He said the
National Coordinator had "goofed," the two figures were
"snafus," and the Campaign was not in any immediate
financial crisis.

At the campsite the sky cleared after several intermittently
rainy days, and construction went on all day Saturday and
into the night. March leaders met again for several hours
with church and city officials about their housing squeeze.
The SCLC staff denied the reports that some churches had
become unhappy or uncooperative with their plans. But the
Midwest Caravan, which arrived that evening, was put up
not in churches but in the Washington Coliseum. By Sunday night, churches in northern Virginia were available for
only the 450 in the Southern Caravan.

Rev. Abernathy flew back to Washington Sunday after
launching the Southwestern Caravan from Albuquerque and
meeting with the General Assembly of the United Presbyterian Church, from which he was to win a pledge of
$100,000. At the Pitts Motel he presided over a midnight
strategy session preparing for the initial demonstrations. One
item not on the agenda at the meeting was the heavy rain at
Resurrection City that afternoon, which had once more
stopped construction, was rapidly turning the green turf
into thick, heavy mud, and had forced cancellation of a
"practice" march to the Capitol.

3

Mud, Delays, Squabbles

In the five and a half weeks from May 12 to June 19, the Campaign was continually prevented from getting off the ground by seemingly inexorable conjunctions of bad luck and mismanagement that afflicted nearly every aspect of the operation. Two factors — the delay of Solidarity Day and the rain — were central to the process.

There had been no time since April to plan ahead for the big support march. When Abernathy returned to Washington on May 19, delaying the rally seemed necessary if it was to have any chance of success at all. Its success was considered important because the out-of-town supporters would be needed when the Campaign thrust turned to nation-wide economic action. To make the most of the additional time, Abernathy asked Bayard Rustin to take over the job of mobilizing the rally.

Rustin had been one of Dr. King's most trusted advisers for some years, and had masterminded the mammoth March on Washington in 1963. Since then he had moved to Dr. King's right, obtaining much of his support from the entrenched hierarchy of organized labor. He now saw change as possible and desirable almost exclusively through a Negro-liberal-labor coalition within the Democratic Party and had been an unremitting opponent of Black Power. Dr. King's

own leftward shift had increased the distance between them.
New York newspapers had reported Rustin earlier in the
year as being sharply critical of Campaign plans, particularly the threat of mass civil disobedience. There was much
opposition within the SCLC inner circle to having him associated with the Campaign, but it was admitted that his
handling of the rally would probably attract to it many white
liberals nearer the political center than SCLC. Rustin, who
was at the Sunday night meeting, agreed to take the job,
and the announcement was made Tuesday, May 21.

The delaying of Solidarity Day produced another very important tactical decision: mass arrests were to be put off until after the big march, because the inevitable disruption and
probable violence accompanying them would scare off many
liberals who preferred their demonstrations to be peaceful
and picnic-like.

This change in tactics was not admitted publicly, but was
evident before long. While effective demonstrations are possible without courting arrests, they require considerable in-
genuity and inventiveness to pull off — much more than do
the simple entering of proscribed areas and the blocking of
doors, which actions generally suffice for a trip to jail. And
unfortunately, SCLC's demonstrations prior to Solidarity Day
were neither ingenious nor inventive. Of approximately 40
marches held during those weeks, most consisted of a trek to
some government agency, the presentation or discussion of
demands with officials, singing, speech-making and finally a
return to the camp. The only significant departures from this
pattern were a few vigils, one at the State Department, one
at the apartment house of House Ways and Means Committee Chairman Wilbur Mills, and a ragged, week-long watch
around the Agriculture Department.

Nor were the demonstrations massive or militant, despite
weekly declarations by Abernathy and other executive staff
members that "the picnic is over" and they were about to

get down to "serious business." Over half the demonstrations involved less than 200 people, and over three-quarters involved less than 325. On only three occasions were arrests made, for a total of less than 40 during this period, and in each case it was clear the arrests were accidental and not part of the demonstration strategy. By Sunday, June 2, few newsmen covering the Campaign and not many of the marchers were paying much attention when Hosea Williams shouted at them, "If the police want to use those clubs we're going to give them a chance to use them tomorrow. I'm telling you that Monday we're gonna start demonstrations that folks on Capitol Hill won't be able to stand. We are ready to bleed as long as there is a drop of blood in us."

The next day Williams led 400 campaigners to the Justice Department, where they stood at the door and haggled for eight hours over whether the Attorney General would see 25 or 100 of their number. No one was arrested.

SCLC's strategists are creative and experienced planners of nonviolent protest, so that the lack of drama was not the result of any paucity of ability. The roots of the problem lay rather in the organizational and physical morass that was Resurrection City after the rains came.

The staff was having a difficult time keeping control of the city even before the first sustained rainfall began May 23. While most of the shantytown residents were docile and uncomplaining, a significant number of young "dudes," many of them urban gang members, were from their arrival constantly getting out of hand, drinking, assaulting other residents and outsiders, harassing newsmen, taunting police and stealing everything that could be lifted. The staff finally lost patience with some of them and in one day, May 22, sent more than 200 home. Those ousted cursed at reporters and bystanders up to the moment they climbed into busses for the return trip. Asked about the reasons for their expulsion,

Bevel admitted, "They went around and beat up on our white people. They interfered with the workers and were hostile to the press. We had to get them out." But the action came too late on both counts: the press had already been disillusioned and the internal unrest, once started, never really died down. More youths were sent home, but some returned and many were replaced by others like them from the Washington area who were attracted by the free food and shelter (such as they were), the sanctuary from police pursuit, and the presence of so many suckers waiting to be hustled.

In the face of this assault from within, most of the SCLC field staff proved helpless or even indifferent. Impressive-sounding programs were said to be planned for the camp — a radio station, cultural and recreational activities, a "poor people's university," a day-care center, etc. — but few of them materialized, even though scores of volunteers were standing by and considerable amounts of money had been donated for them. Only the top people — Jesse Jackson, James Bevel, Hosea Williams, Andy Young, and Abernathy — could control the hell-raisers even temporarily, and all of these men spent far more time then they admitted breaking up fights and cooling off drunken attacks on the police outside the fence. By forcing everyone to stay inside, the rains masked the problem somewhat; but each time the sun came out, the trouble emerged along with it.

Whatever small relief the rain brought by dampening the city's more disorderly residents, it more than swept away in a flood of new problems. The same staff members who showed themselves incapable of dealing with the camp's rowdies were likewise unequal to the mud. Four times in three weeks the campsite was reduced to a barely passable stretch of viscous mire; each of the first three times was thought to be the last, and few serious measures were taken to make the succeeding downpours less devastating. The easygoing, always-muddling-through disorganization for which

SCLC is famous became here a maddening and embittering chaos.

Despite these increasingly apparent shortcomings, conference leaders regularly explained to the press that things were really falling into place and finally getting organized. On May 31, for example, Andrew Young told a typically late press conference that Rev. Abernathy's quarters had now been completed (which they had not), and that the job of getting the tent city organized was "almost finished." The camp's near-readiness, he went on, would free top staff members to mobilize black Washington, along with ghettoes in the nearby cities of Baltimore, Richmond, and Philadelphia, to support the movement. It would also, he said, make it possible to begin transferring the administrative work of running Resurrection City from the SCLC staff to the residents and their representatives. Similar statements were made five more times during the next two weeks.

A further drain on the leadership's time were the interethnic squabbles, primarily between the Mexican-Americans and SCLC, which began as soon as the Southwestern Caravan arrived in Washington May 23. The most vociferous among these later arrivals was New Mexico's Reies Lopez Tijerina.

Mr. Tijerina is the leader of a group he calls The Political Confederation of Free City-States in the Southwest. The organization is based on an interpretation of the 1848 Treaty of Guadalupe-Hidalgo, by which Mexico ceded most of the Southwest to the United States. Tijerina contends the treaty guaranteed the Spanish land grants, running into millions of acres, of families then living there, and that the federal government had taken this land away in violation of the treaty. The treaty also, says Tijerina, provided for the preservation of the natives' language and culture, provisions which he asserts have also been disregarded.

Mr. Tijerina was new to nonviolence. He and his followers

dramatized their complaints at home with guns, staging what amounted to insurrections by running state and local officials out of territory they felt was theirs and electing their own government to replace them. These uprisings left a bundle of criminal indictments hanging over Tijerina's head in New Mexico, though he was cleared of one after a trial in October 1968.

Without question the fiery Southwestern rebel regarded the Poor People's Campaign as an unparalleled opportunity to gain nationwide attention for his cause. It is not so easy to determine what commitment he had to the Campaign's objectives of ending hunger and poverty. In public he showed little interest in SCLC's demands concerning food stamps, jobs, housing, guaranteed incomes, etc. The treaty and the land were the subjects of all his speeches. Getting the land back — or at least obtaining a cash settlement of the claims — *that* would solve his people's problems.

Some conflict between Tijerina and SCLC appears to have been almost inevitable. On the way to Washington, he and the other Mexican-Americans had walked out of a rally in Kansas City on May 19, complaining that the rally's program was exclusively black and run mostly by local black leaders. The Mexican-Americans returned to the meeting after Rodolfo "Corky" Gonzalez of Denver was made Master of Ceremonies. The Mexican-Americans were a much more tightly knit and disciplined group than most of the residents of Resurrection City. They arrived just as the shantytown was sinking under the first heavy onslaught of rain, and were quartered "temporarily" at Hawthorne School, a private experimental secondary school in southwest D.C. The school, though crowded, was dry and warm, and the families in the group rapidly lost interest in moving out into the mud. Tijerina soon discovered that the threat of not moving into the campsite at all was a useful tool in getting what he felt was his share of attention from the Campaign leadership and the press. It was a tool he did not hesitate to use.

Tijerina's most frequent complaint was that the SCLC leadership did not take the needs and opinions of non-black groups sufficiently into account in making decisions. SCLC officials privately replied to the claim with some asperity. They believe Tijerina had virtually no interest in the Campaign beyond its use to him as a forum for his land claims, and they say he was impossible to work with. Abernathy, they feel, went out of his way to accommodate the Mexican-Americans and Indians, and they point in evidence to the march he led — with Tijerina and the Indians — to the Supreme Court on May 29, in protest of its decision affirming limitations on Indian fishing rights in certain rivers of Washington State. Abernathy reportedly felt the demonstration to be very bad tactics — as several subsequent newspaper editorials took pains to assure him — because of the generally favorable trend of high court civil rights decisions, but he had agreed to join it as a gesture of solidarity with the other ethnic groups and their demands. The march did turn out badly: bored campaigners began throwing each other into the Court Plaza's stately fountains, several windows got broken, and five persons were arrested in an ambiguous, unplanned confrontation with police.

The SCLC account of top-level efforts to take the other ethnic groups into consideration is impressive. But anyone familiar with the organization knows that its top-level staff operate in many ways like a large, closely knit family (other, less friendly observers have called it simply a self-interested clique). They have been accustomed to dominating a movement situation, not necessarily by conscious manipulation but by the overpowering moral stature of their late leader, which generally has awed local leaders, especially Negro preachers and white liberals, into agreement with their plans. And the executives' relationships with lower staff members tend

to be paternalistic. It is thus easy to suspect that sharing decision-making with other groups was not something that
came naturally to them. The most plausible explanation of
the difficulties between the Conference and Tijerina would
probably be to see the New Mexican as highly sensitive to
any evidence, real or imagined, of being left out, and the
Conference leaders as earnestly trying to take others into
account but slipping back frequently into the old ways.

It was widely suspected and even assumed in the press
at this time that the Campaign's progress was being further
impeded by a behind-the-scenes struggle for power within
SCLC. The suggestion was that Rev. Abernathy's leadership
was being undercut by others in the group's executive staff
who felt that he was inadequate as Dr. King's successor.
Those most often mentioned as the contenders for his power
were Executive Vice President Andrew J. Young and the
Action Director, Hosea Williams. These reports were largely
a combination of wishful thinking and misinterpretation of
what was happening. There were undoubtedly vigorous conflicts within the executive staff; long-standing clashes of personality and differences in strategic thinking have dogged
SCLC for years. These conflicts may have intensified after
Dr. King's death; moreover, the executive staff was divided
over many tactical decisions during the Campaign: Hosea
Williams disagreed with the whole Resurrection City idea;
most of the staff was very skeptical of Bayard Rustin's role;
there was argument about accepting surplus foods offered
by the government to feed the campers. But this kind of
vehement debate is virtually a characteristic of SCLC de-
liberations, and does not provide any substantive evidence of
a power struggle.

The persistent inclination to interpret these internal dy-
namics as efforts to supplant Abernathy reflects in my opinion
a reluctance on the part of those holding it to accept as Dr.
King's successor a man whose public personality has not been

designed to fit their image of The Responsible Negro Leader. As we have seen, Ralph Abernathy was cut from sturdy but much rougher cloth than his cultured and patrician predecessor. Where Dr. King's image among white liberals and the press was carefully and painstakingly cultivated, Abernathy had not sought and was not given much attention until leadership was thrust upon him. As he struggled in those weeks to establish himself as a leader in his own right as well as Dr. King's heir, many whites, especially among the press, were put off by his unpolished, sometimes abrasive and seemingly indecisive manner. It was not surprising that some newsmen began looking to other members of Dr. King's circle, whom they felt they understood better, and attributing to them qualities that would calm their unease. Thus the mention of Andrew Young, an urbane, well-bred and lightskinned man, one of whose major duties was dealing with white leaders and the press; similarly Hosea Williams, whose Malcolm X goatee and extravagantly angry rhetoric fitted him well into the manageable stereotype of the "militant" trying to elbow aside more moderate spokesmen. But these two men, along with the other top staff members, repeatedly and emphatically affirmed their loyalty to Abernathy in public and private. It is possible that some of them may eventually leave SCLC for other pursuits; but it is highly unlikely that any of them spent time during the Campaign plotting the overthrow of their new leader.

All these forces, after two weeks of mud and unimpressive marches, combined into a turning point for the Campaign on June 6. The rain had temporarily given over to Washington's other type of summer weather: thick, enervating heat and cloying humidity, as uncomfortable in its way as the rain had been. Resurrection City's population, which had peaked at about 2,500 on May 26, was now down to around 500. Some hundreds of people had been sent home,

but many more had found the tepid demonstrations insufficient compensation for the problems of mud, confusion, theft,
and assault that dogged the shantytown, and they had simply
gone back home. Senator Robert Kennedy, shot in California
two nights earlier after wining the state's presidential primary,
had just died. Senator Kennedy was the most popular white
political leader in the nation among black people, and the
SCLC leadership had reportedly been giving serious consideration to endorsing his presidential candidacy, a move
without precedent in the organization's history.

The shooting had been indirectly responsible for one of
the most public and embarrassing disputes yet between the
SCLC leadership and Reies Tijerina. The New Mexican
had been planning for several days to demonstrate at the
State Department on June 5. But when he announced the
formation of the march to a crowd outside Resurrection City
that afternoon, he was interrupted by Hosea Williams, who
said he knew nothing of this march, that all march plans had
to be cleared with him as Action Director and that *he* had
decided to picket the National Rifle Association for its opposition to gun control. Tijerina replied that his march had been
approved by the Campaign Steering Committee the day before. The exchange, which included personal insults, went on
for several more rounds, with Tijerina castigating the SCLC
leadership for leaving his group out of Campaign decision-
making and Williams finally making vague conciliatory remarks in an effort to get the altercation away from the large
audience of fascinated reporters and angry marchers it had
attracted. Williams changed his plans later that afternoon
and led a group of 150 to the Office of Economic Opportunity,
while Tijerina walked defiantly on with 30 others to the State
Department, which was surrounded for the occasion by a
force of one hundred policemen.

That evening, the heat once more brought out into the
open the camp's internal turbulence. Several fights had

broken out the night before, and bigger, bloodier brawls oc-
curred in the dining tent that afternoon, throwing the population into an uproar. A town meeting was called outside the
snow fence near the Reflecting Pool, where a stage and am-
plifiers had been set up. The location proved unfortunate,
because in addition to the somber gray statue of Lincoln
watching reflectively from across Memorial Circle, dozens
of less detached tourists and newsmen gathered to hear the
acrimonious debate that ensued.

One angry black woman took the mike to anounce that
she was from Chicago and had quit her job to come here
with her nine sons and daughters. "And if any of you men
lay a hand on one of my daughters," she shouted, "I swear
to God I'll kill you *dead!*" She let go of the mike as if finished, then grabbed it again to add "And I'm *nonviolent!*"
A tall man in marshal's denims said he was tired of the
hassles and thought it was time some residents put down
their wine bottles and knives long enough to remember
why they were here. A thin fellow in a SNCC sweatshirt
asked a series of snide rhetorical questions about why the
staff continued to stay at the Pitts Motel. When a rough-look-
ing, scarfaced man approached the mike, he was met by scat-
tered jeers. The impression one got was that he had been
involved in the afternoon's fighting, and was trying to respond to the marshal's complaints. But he only spoke a few
sentences, punctuated by louder boos from the audience,
before throwing the mike away and shouting in rage, *"God-
dammit,* I don't have to talk to *you* sons*abitches!"* The most
affecting speaker was a young, troubled black man who ar-
ticulated what was on many minds. He had come, he said,
to be used by the leadership in a campaign against poverty.
He was ready to face the authorities and to go to jail —
anxious to go in fact; but there had been no real action so
far, and that, he believed, was why there was so much

trouble in the camp. When, he wanted to know, would the action start? When could the people go to jail?

No one answered his questions; and a few moments later, with the crowd still upset and angered, an SCLC field organizer named Benjamin Van Clarke announced that the meeting was moving inside Resurrection City because too many outsiders were mingling with the assembly around the platform.

Rev. Abernathy was waiting inside the fence to speak to the people. He promised them fried chicken and Coca-Cola by the weekend and explained again why the job of fund-raising and overall Campaign coordination made it necessary for him to stay in a motel rather than at the campsite. If he spent all his time at Resurrection City, he said, he could not be the leader he had to be. "And which do you want," he asked them, "a leader who *sleeps* with you, or a leader who *leads* you?" Those crowded around him mechanically shouted assent at the proper times. But other citizens who had gathered instead in their own groups were not listening. Abernathy did not explain why there had been no action, or indicate when it would begin and his talk thus did little to calm the seething shantytown; those who caused most of the trouble drifted away, muttering contemptuously to each other that the SCLC president was "talkin' nothin' but a lotta shit."

Abernathy's intentions were good, but it did seem that for too many staff members the bourgeois comforts of the Pitts Motel were much more attractive than the mud and rudeness of Resurrection City. Yet they retained most of the policy-making positions, leaving the camp with an intolerable lack of dependable on-the-scene leadership.

One result of this was the continuing failure of mechanisms, like the City Council, which were ostensibly designed to make possible participation by the campaigners in decision-making. This gave rise to angry comments like the following by Wolfe Lowenthal in the September 1968 issue of *Liberation*: "SCLC has a heavy paternalistic attitude toward its followers. When a demonstration was called the word would come blaring out over the P.A. system. . . . A great deal of the time you didn't know where it was you were going, or why, or what you were going to do once you got there." Writing in the same pages, author Barbara Deming, who also lived in the camp, was less angry but in agreement about what happened: "Here was a situation that called above all for everyone to be listening to the thoughts of others. SCLC leaders were both too exhausted to do so and too used to being the ones to be listened to rather than to listen. If this had not been so, I think that the people there in the city could have suggested to them how to stage a demonstration that would not have been quickly forgotten by this country." Since they had been told little of the Campaign's strategy beyond the need to come to Washington and the likelihood of going to jail, the people's frustrations were predictable, as was the probability of their coming to the fore again. Late the next night, a group of Commandos, activist black teenagers from Milwaukee whose leader is the militant white priest, Father James Groppi, invaded the Pitts Motel to demand that the staff vacate their expensive rooms and join them in the caking mud of West Potomac Park. All they managed to do was find Hosea Williams and engage him in an extended, futile shouting match.

On June 6 all these currents were coming together to wash away the leadership's hope of focussing national attention on the realities of hunger and poverty. And as if they weren't sufficient to distract the public from the issues, Bayard Rustin assured their effect by announcing that afternoon that he was suspending his work of mobilizing for Solidarity Day and giving Rev. Abernathy twenty-four hours to "clarify" his role or accept his resignation.

Rustin's move was not entirely a surprise. On June 2 he

had issued a revised list of Campaign demands which he said had "the complete authority" of Rev. Abernathy. The specific legislative demands were reformist, calling for one million federally financed jobs, passage of a pending housing bill, repeal of Wilbur Mills' welfare amendments, extension of labor laws to farm workers, restoration of budget cuts in various poverty programs, and a Presidential declaration of national emergency, which would make possible administrative action to beef up social programs. To these were appended a call for a vague governmental commitment to an "economic bill of rights" that guaranteed all citizens a job or an income.

The list was hailed by editors and liberal politicians as an important refinement of the Campaign's sweeping rhetoric into concrete, attainable objectives that could be fitted into conventional political bargaining processes. But within the SCLC executive staff, the list was not greeted with pleasure. Emerging from a strategy meeting on June 4, Hosea Williams blasted it as "a bunch of jazz and foolishness. Bayard Rustin was given the job of doing some public relations work for the big day on the 19th and nothing else. The policy statement is completely out of order...we do not accept it and I'm sure the steering committee will reject it." Later in the day Abernathy told newsmen in Miami that he "did not authorize and neither did [he] issue" the policy statement. "I do not think it is comprehensive enough to cover the demands of the Poor People's Campaign. I go along with some of his ideas but I think it's got to be much broader." When pressed as to what more it should include, he mentioned only a condemnation of the war in Vietnam, but later added that another significant omission was the lack of any mention of land claims or fishing rights, the specific demands of the Mexican-American and Indian participants. Relations between the ethnic groups were sensitive just then, and men like Tijerina could be expected to react sharply to policy statements which neglected their concerns.

Rustin's press secretary, when informed of the reaction, replied that he had read the statement to Andrew Young and had his approval. Abernathy retorted calmly that Rev. Young did not have final authority in such matters, and the dispute hung unresolved until Rustin's move on Thursday. The staff was clearly ready for Rustin's action. The twenty-four hour deadline passed without public comment, then Abernathy told a press conference he had accepted the resignation with regret, calling the incident a "minor misunderstanding."

Thus on June 6 Rustin was on his way out. His departure, after the leadership's rejection of what the press had regarded as an important contribution, combined with a vicious assault on two reporters on the perimeter of the campsite that night, seemed suddenly to crystallize all the reporters' misgivings about the Campaign into a spurt of critical copy. Newspapers were dotted for days with headlines like the following. June 8: "Confused Goals," an editorial in the *Evening Star,* and "Poor Camp: A City Adrift," in the *Washington Post.* June 9: "Campaign in Trouble," in the *New York Times,* "Leadership Crisis Perils Poor March" and "Poor People's Campaign Nearing Fiasco," both in the *Post.* June 10: "Dissent Jeopardizes the Poor People's Campaign," in the *Christian Science Monitor.* June 11: "Confusion Obscures Poor People's Specific Demands," in the *Post.* June 12: "Discontent Mounts at Resurrection City, More Leaving," in the *Star.*

There was considerable factual basis for most of these stories. But they also made clear that the press attitude at all levels, which had been shifting from cautious support, through confusion, into ambivalence, was settling firmly into a consistent and critical, almost cynical stance. Once established, such a mood is very difficult to dislodge, either from the newsmen who have it or their readers and listeners who usually accept it. By the end of the next week, the Campaign had clearly lost the sympathy of an essential ally, and was thereafter constantly on the defensive.

SCLC stuck to its strategy, and its response to the press criticism was meager. James Bevel, speaking to a mass meeting in Washington's ghetto on June 7, characterized press reports of the inter-ethnic problems as part of white America's scheme to keep poor people divided and ineffective. Mr. Sterling Tucker, Director of Washington's Urban League, accepted Rustin's post after some hesitation. Otherwise it was business as usual: all marches were called off during the period of mourning for Senator Kennedy; but then "a new phase" of "more meaningful" demonstrations was said to be imminent. Hosea Williams announced that several competing groups of marshals at Resurrection City were merging into one larger unit to streamline the camp's security situation; then he withdrew the announcement when the groups made it embarrassingly clear they did not plan to merge with anybody. At Hawthorne School, the Mexican-Americans were still voicing dissatisfaction with their treatment. And on Monday, June 10, the rains returned.

4

Solidarity Day

The week of June 10 began in a by now familiar pattern: plans were still uncertain as the Campaign's "Action Committee" met for hours, there was an unenlightening press conference, more expressions of discontent were heard from the Mexican-Americans, and heavy rainstorms battered the campsite in the afternoon. Sixty residents of Resurrection City finally straggled to the Health, Education and Welfare Department before the day was over to complain that their welfare checks for May and June had not been forwarded from home.

The new phase of "more meaningful" demonstrations was announced on Tuesday morning and turned out to be a call for around-the-clock picketing at the Agriculture Department, which was promptly delayed until Wednesday by more rain. The vigil was to focus attention on the Campaign's special concern for ending hunger, which the leadership insisted could be largely accomplished by vigorous departmental action without major new legislation.

Tuesday night, Abernathy amplified this focus on hunger, releasing a 23-item summary list of demands at a second, extended press briefing. The list called for three legislative actions: passage of Pennsylvania Sen. Joseph Clark's jobs bill, the pending 5 billion dollar housing bill, and repeal of Wilbur Mills' welfare amendments. The other 20 items were administrative actions beefing up federal welfare and poverty programs and making them more responsive to the needs and wishes of the poor. Heavy emphasis was laid on the expansion of food stamp and surplus food distribution programs into poor counties which did not have them, as well as the issuance of free food stamps to persons too poor to buy them. The summary also included one demand apiece from the Indians and Mexican-Americans, calling on the State Department to address the issue of the land claims, and upon the Interior Department to improve education, health and job conditions on reservations.

Abernathy said the marchers would concentrate on the administrative demands until Solidarity Day, then take aim on the Congress with the legislative proposals. He also hinted broadly that if these demands were met the leadership would consider them substantial enough victories to bring the Campaign to a close. What he did not say was that the list represented a major scaling down of the movement's objectives: it did not mention the war in Vietnam and placed the enactment of guaranteed job and income programs under the lower priority heading of actions to be undertaken for fiscal 1969. In fact, the list varied only slightly in its specifics and not much more in emphasis from Bayard Rustin's call, and it strongly suggests that the leadership was now considering ways of covering their tracks if the Campaign did not generate the public pressure to get what it wanted from Congress.

Overall Campaign tactics, however, were still being programmed according to the original rough scenario. The pickets at Agriculture tramped around the building for a week, beginning in the heaviest rain of their stay. Resurrection City, again awash, came close to being abandoned after 2.23 inches of precipitation fell on it in 24 hours June 12 and 13. James Bevel, who had worked primarily at the campsite during its first two weeks, was now conducting three mass meetings a week out in the D.C. ghettoes, each at a different church, preaching the importance to the movement's success of black Washington's participation and directing efforts to mobilize local groups into a readiness to move when the leadership needed them.

While Abernathy was telling white audiences repeatedly that if the Campaign did not succeed they could expect black people to turn to riots and violence as the means of inducing change, Bevel was taking a somewhat different approach in the District's black churches. "If there is not a Poor People's Campaign," he told a small, astonished audience in the black middle-class Deanwood section, "you are goin' to get polarization of the races, and you are goin' to get niggers wiped *out*. Y'all hear me? Y'all better say amen."

The amens sounded unconvinced, but Bevel did not spare his listeners' feelings in explaining how this could happen:

"Now you can sit here and play jive if you want to like you don't know what the hell's goin' on. But I said, that if the [white] community becomes sufficiently fearful, in order to relieve its anxiety it will kill [black] folks off, without any thought about it. . . .

"When fear becomes sufficient in a Hitler's Germany, they will murder off Jews in an attempt to eliminate their own anxiety. . . . Johnson says he's gotta train 200,000 soldiers for the ghettoes — to clean up the streets? or to spill blood? And we're sittin' around playin' dead, duckin', pretending like we're into somethin', and we're facing annihilation.

"Now y'all better get hep. The problem with the Jews, they sat around playin' dumb: 'Oh, Hitler's gonna miss *me*.' They said, 'He ain't gonna get me because I'm workin' for the government. . . .'

"Now when I listen to these guys runnin' around here talkin' about 'kill whitey, blah blah blah blah' — you think they frighten the Pentagon? The people in the Pentagon are

militarists: they deal in the science of killing. Now a man
who got tommyguns, tanks, mace, napalm, rockets, sleeping
gas...who can put a fence around the ghetto in about 2
hours any day they want to, they ain't gonna hardly be
excited over Stokely Carmichael cussin'. But what Carmichael does with this kind of foolishness is frighten the white
populace, which gives the militarists the license to do what
they wanna do. Do y'all hear what I'm sayin? It gives them
the license to do what they wanna do; because once they can
say, 'Oh, I'm savin' y'all, the niggers gon' get y'all,' they have
the license to kill. And if anxiety grows deep enough and
big enough, in order to eliminate their anxiety they'll have to
kill you....Now if you think they killed the Vietnamese,
you let there become some racial polarization: they will fry
niggers on the White House steps—I know 'em—because
they are pathological killers and they cannot help it. Y'all
hear me? All right. Now they just went all across the country
and killed off the buffalo, murdered the Indians, murdered
the Vietnamese, killed 50 million Africans—you know, Johnson wakes up and just gets orgasms when he hears 'I killed
a *thousand* men last night in Vietnam'....He's *happy;* you
understand what I mean—that man is *sick*....He's just
killin' up folks, eatin' barbecue.

"That's why we have to have a Poor People's Campaign,
to redirect the minds and the attention of the American
people onto economics. Our scheme is to take a section of
all the communities, black and white, and say, 'No, no, the
issue is not black versus white, the issue is a new economic
order.' Now that's why I'm walkin' around down in the mud,
callin' in Negroes from all over the country, Indians, Puerto
Ricans and white folks, to say the issue is an economy that
deals with the development of the minds of its people."

Bevel hammered at this theme again and again; and along
with it, the importance of mobilizing Washington to join
with the movement if it was to be a success:

"We got about 500 people in Resurrection City, which simply means that the 500 people must become teachers and preachers.... We must get out in Washington and work: talk to people in Washington, knock on doors in Washington, mobilize people in Washington. Resurrection City cannot remain an island; it must become a church that goes out into Washington and moves Washington to fight for the poor.... We must demonstrate every day, but in the afternoon we must get out into Washington ... we must come back and canvass, knock on doors, talkin' to people about the reality of poverty in this country."

Bevel's speeches at mass meetings showed increasing concern with this mobilization of Washington as Solidarity Day came nearer. The Administration, which seemed content to let the Campaign sink into the mud, was coming under increasing Congressional pressure to clear the Park of the campers. Several bills to outlaw gatherings on public property had been introduced in the House as the Campaign made its way to Washington. One of these, a bill by Florida Representative William Cramer which barred further permits for the Campaign after the initial expiration date of June 16 and established a joint House-Senate Grievance Committee to hear citizen complaints, had made its way through the House Subcommittee on Public Buildings and Grounds and on June 5 was cleared for floor debate by the Rules Comittee. As the Campaign floundered through the next week, its Congressional opponents used the threat of this bill's passage to force the administration's hand in negotiations between the Park Service and SCLC over a permit for Solidarity Day and an extension for Resurrection City. Senator Robert Byrd of West Virginia, chairman of the District Appropriations Subcommittee which would handle the Cramer bill in the upper house, had opposed the original permit and repeatedly criticized the Campaign. But he postponed any action on the bill and agreed to a one-week extension when Parks Director Nash Castro assured him the new deadline of June 23 would be final. SCLC requested a 30-day extension, but the Park Service decision, announced Friday June 14, only granted the week's extension. Rev. Abernathy commented that he felt further one-week extensions would be forthcoming, and insisted the marchers would stay in their camp, permit or no permit.

The possibility of the camp being closed and the residents carried out was obviously on the leadership's mind as it continued to press for support from the people in Washington. It was also clear by mid-month that the response of the area's black people was not what was hoped for. Abernathy was perplexed when he spoke on June 12 to a meeting of support groups for Solidarity Day: "Everywhere I've gone," he said, "I've found more white people than black people. . . . I don't know why we're not reaching black people. I understand that the majority of the [Washington] population is black. But somehow we are not reaching them."

At few of the mass meetings were the churches crowded, and the audiences, while mostly enthusiastic, were not wildly so. The contrast between these meetings and those of the 1965 Selma Campaign, for example, was stark. In Selma, meetings were held six nights a week for almost ten weeks, and virtually every night the church was jammed — platforms, aisles, balconies and doorways — an hour early by people who shook the rafters and walls with tumultuous stomping, clapping and singing responses to their leaders' exhortations. Few left the meetings not feeling exhilarated and strengthened in commitment to the movement's cause — and to its leaders and their strategy as well. The Washington meetings, though held less often and with a much larger black population to draw from, never produced responses of comparable intensity or size. Only one meeting, shortly after Solidarity Day, approached the same exciting atmosphere, and as we shall see it was an isolated instance.

This tepid response is difficult to account for with pre-
cision; but two characteristics of successful movements can
be projected which may provide some perspective. First of
all, successful movements of SCLC's style must appear as
the untainted champions of an undoubtedly moral cause doing battle against an acknowledged evil, preferably represented by a villain figure like Jim Clark or Bull Connor. But
the disorganization and violence at Resurrection City, combined with the embarrassing interethnic quarrels, grossly
compromised the leadership's image. Moreover, as Abernathy
himself confessed to the National Press Club on June 15,
the Campaign had tried and failed to find on Capitol Hill a
villain who would make the offensive public gestures which
could stir up national opinion and focus it outside the be-
leaguered, muddy campsite. They had tried to settle on Agriculture Secretary Orville Freeman; but he was the essence of
courteous, concerned officialdom, visiting with the marchers
and assuring them he was doing everything he possibly could.
House Ways and Means Chairman Mills, whose 1967 welfare amendments were indeed villainous, was next; but he
was such a colorless and elusive character that one evening
he slipped unnoticed right past a line of angry welfare pickets
into his Connecticut Avenue apartment house. And Senator
James O. Eastland, whose plantations collect better than
$200,000 annually in government subsidies for not farming
while starving black children on welfare in his home Mississippi county are allotted $9.00 each per month, somehow
remained completely beyond the reach of the marchers' moral
floodlight.

A second factor probably affecting black Washington's
response was the Campaign's equally uncertain performance
as entertainment. An effective movement of this type must
be not only morally commanding, but also dramatic and exciting — it must be the best show in town. It was this excite-
ment and motion that made previous movements able to

absorb and neutralize otherwise disruptive elements of their constituencies. During the height of the Montgomery Bus Boycott of 1956, juvenile delinquency in the black community virtually disappeared. Likewise in Selma: many persons whose main occupations were known to be alcohol, fisticuffs, and wenching left these pastimes behind to join the movement, standing in the rain for days on end beside nuns and white college students, going to jail, etc. Once the activity was over most of these people returned to their former pursuits, as juvenile delinquency no doubt returned to black Montgomery; but both they and the victorious campaigns had profited from their participation.

The Poor People's Campaign not only failed to generate a similar dramatic hold on the local community, it was for a month after its arrival in Washington rather dull. Hosea Williams complained to newsmen that they were "engaged in a conspiracy to poison the mind of America" against the Campaign. When they entered Resurrection City, he insisted that "most look only at what's bad. They sneak around like an underground assassin, looking for dirt and filth." There may indeed have been ulterior motives in some of the negative reportage, but it should be evident by now that most newsmen had lost their enthusiasm for the Campaign after repeated frustrations and rebuffs; and even for the few remaining friendly observers there was little of interest to write about in that first month beyond the Campaign's problems. In public the leadership was coy and vague about its strategy until the very end. The pre-Solidarity Day demonstrations quickly became such a crashing bore that covering them was the oppressive drudgery that will kill a newsman's sympathy with his subject as quickly as anything. Viewed from without, confusion seemed to reign so completely over the Campaign that the hostility and internal quarreling appeared as its most consistent characteristics.

These same impressions were undoubedly left in the minds

of many local blacks who visited the camp, as well as hundreds of thousands more who encountered it through the media. Some were skeptical of it, most were indifferent, and the parasites who moved into the camp were left to try their luck with little to distract them.

Mass meetings and canvassing were not enough to counteract the movement's faltering image. The SCLC preachers seemed to sense this lack of rapport, and their performances in the pulpit were not the finest. James Bevel, an orator without peer when at his best, was strained and repetitive, leaning more than normally on emotional phrases, like "sick, pathological killers," and sophistical flights of logic. Rev. Abernathy, throughout this period, always looked exhausted and had yet to regain the eloquence he commanded when Dr. King was alive. Only the young Rev. Jesse Jackson, director of Operation Breadbasket, spoke regularly with fluency and force. But he was not enough. Black Washington, on the eve of Solidarity Day was not moving with the Campaign.

After its soggy, stumbling start, the Agriculture vigil seemed to inspire some new enthusiasm in the remaining residents of the tent city. Thursday, June 13, as 300 of them filled the sidewalks and surrounded the two-square block complex with protest, Abernathy was prompted to observe, "This campaign is really gaining momentum and everything is falling into place." The spirits of the protesters were boosted again Friday by news of the arrest of 110 members of the Campaign Mule Train 30 miles west of Atlanta. Among those arrested were young sons of Abernathy and Hosea Williams. The jailings were a whiff of the action most vigilers had hoped to find in Washington and it gave them a lift that kept enthusiasm up through the weekend.

Perhaps taking advantage of this burst of fervor, Abernathy and the staff disappeared on Friday from their rooms at the Pitts Motel. The move, not discovered by the press until

Monday, was explained in a letter from Abernathy to the motel's owner as being necessary: "It is mandatory that we move into Resurrection City immediately because of the urgency of our Campaign." Neither he nor many others on the staff moved into the camp, however, and reporters for *The Evening Star* soon located groups of them registered at the Washington Hilton and a Howard Johnson motor lodge; Rev. Abernathy was reported to be staying in a private residence in the city.

The picketers at the Agriculture complex were unaware of these events uptown. Monday afternoon of the 17th their lines, again soaked by an afternoon cloudburst, spontaneously broke into small groups that began blocking doors to the building, a disruption Departmental officials were not ready to permit. The blockade continued for more than an hour. But just as police began moving into position and arrests seemed imminent, Hosea Williams arrived to call the marchers off, telling them, "We're not ready for mass jailing. Maybe we will be ready tomorrow."

Tuesday several were arrested, but only inadvertently, after the Agriculture vigil was called off to support a demonstration by the National Welfare Rights Organization near the White House. The welfare group had obtained an appointment for Tuesday afternoon with Wilbur Mills, but it was cancelled because the Chairman was still in a committee meeting. The group decided to march three miles up Connecticut Avenue to Mills' residence, and the 9 arrests came when several persons tried to cross police lines to join the march.

The ragtag files moved slowly up the Avenue past some of Washington's more fashionable places of business and pleasure, giving well-dressed couples at tiny sidewalk cafe tables something novel to smile and giggle about over their pre-dinner drinks. When they finally arrived, the several hundred marchers nearly surrounded the drab yellowbrick apartment house where Mills resided. A multitude of police ringed the building, and their captain repeatedly ordered the protesters to keep moving. Faces, mostly old, appeared behind the dark screens of several windows, peering down uneasily on the chanting demonstrators below. A white-haired man who said he represented the building's owners paced up and down behind the police lines. He told newsmen the demonstrations were upsetting many tenants, particularly older ones, and had the landlord worried. After circling the building once, the marchers stood along the sidewalks singing and listening to impromptu denunciations of the Chairman.

It was then that from the alley in back, Wilbur Mills and his wife walked quietly past police lines up the side of the building and were escorted to a side basement door by a policeman. They had difficulty getting the door to open but none of the pickets and only a few newsmen recognized him and realized what was going on. After some delay the door finally opened and Mills disappeared inside. Out in front, the speeches went on for an hour or so; then the marchers, ready for their dinner, got into busses and headed back to the campsite.

The next day, Wednesday, June 19, was Solidarity Day. Sterling Tucker and a small volunteer staff had, in the space of only ten days, done their job efficiently and well; by sunup busses and cars were arriving in the capital with the first of a swelling crowd. The sky, mercifully, was clear and the city peaceful — though District officials sought to reassure the still nervous area whites by having every available policeman on duty along with 500 police reserves and 1,100 National Guardsmen, and by pointing out that federal troops at nearby bases were on "high alert," just in case.

By noon the grass around the Washington Monument was jammed with people eating sack lunches, listening to the big-name entertainment at nearby Sylvan Theatre, wandering around, or just lounging. Police and press estimates of the crowd's size ranged from 50 to 100,000; Sterling Tucker remarked that the crowd looked fully as large as the 225,000 that gathered there in 1963. Soon the people were moving down past the Reflecting Pool towards the pillared Memorial where Lincoln sat and the program was to be held.

With the clear afternoon came Washington's fierce heat. The early speakers were mostly tedious and everyone was interrupted repeatedly by the screaming jets. The perspiring crowd peaked and soon began thinning out. Hundreds took off their shoes, and ignoring instructions from the podium to stay out of the water, waded into the Reflecting Pool to cool off and have a little frolic.

Comparisons and contrasts with the 1963 march were unavoidable. The crowd was drawn from many of the same groups — churches, unions, and older civil rights groups, though SNCC and CORE were not represented this time. Where the previous march had been an unprecedented event on which the country's attention was focussed for days, this gathering was dwarfed by national convulsions that as recently as two weeks earlier had left the nation emotionally drained. Almost every speaker today was more militant than anyone at the earlier rally had dared to be. Perhaps the most striking difference was in the attitudes of the marchers. Few seemed optimistic about the rally's chances of having much impact. One got the impression they came out of a sense of duty, and once there they were a little bored.

Since 1968, unlike 1963, was an election year, scores of politicians circulated on and around the VIP platform, elbowing marchers and each other to be photographed shaking the important hands — especially that of Mrs. Martin Luther King. As James Bevel was shrilly telling the crowd how important it was for Washington to get behind the movement in the days to come, a major contender for the Democratic Presidential nomination, Senator Eugene McCarthy of Min-

nesota, slipped through the thick shrubbery south of the
Memorial's steps and took a seat well below the platform
behind a fence of Secret Service men. As was his custom,
McCarthy did not seek out the rally's notables, but sat quietly
and let them come to him with their handshakes, which they
did in a steady stream. Photographers swooped in towards
him, only to be met by the ubiquitous campaign marshals
shouting at them to stay away. The photographers were used
to this by now and dodged around the marshals or retreated
a safe distance to use zoom lenses; but the skirmishes continued until Andrew Young worked his way down the Memorial steps and called the marshals off.

A few minutes later, while Mrs. Peggy Terry, a white
"hillbilly" woman from Chicago's Appalachian ghetto, was
explaining how her people were almost as much oppressed
as the city's blacks, Vice President Hubert Humphrey, Mc-
Carthy's front-running rival for the nomination, appeared
from the same bushes to join the Senator in the stands.
The Minnesotans greeted each other with apparent warmth
and spent several moments in quiet conversation.

Dr. Benjamin Mays, President Emeritus of Morehouse College, stepped to the microphone and told the crowd of the
candidates' presence. The mention of Humphrey's name
evoked tepid applause mixed equally with strenuous boos;
McCarthy's applause was also mild at first, started to fade,
then suddenly surged back into a loud, sustained ovation.
Humphrey gave no sign of noticing the difference; but soon
he was up, mounting the steps to pump Mrs. King's hand
and arrange a tableau for photographers with several black
youngsters. Then he disappeared into the Memorial with his
escorts.

McCarthy sat calmly through this display, perhaps even
listening as a big welfare mother stridently denounced every
bureaucrat in Washington and Walter Reuther said all the
right things. At length he rose and made his way back

through the shrubbery toward a waiting limousine. People
saw him crossing the grass and those nearby cheered and
rushed forward to greet him. After shaking a few hands,
McCarthy turned toward his car. But the crowd kept massing
and cheering behind the police line, and he hesitated for a
moment, watching them; but then with a wave, he climbed
into the car and was gone.

It was five o'clock by the time Mrs. King, one of the two
featured speakers, came forward to speak, and the crowd
along the Reflecting Pool had dissipated to the point where
there was more grass showing than people. The maddening
jets were coming almost every minute now; between them
she read a telegram of greeting from Mrs. Robert Kennedy,
then launched into an off-key rendition of the spiritual
"Come By Here, My Lord." That finished, she spoke of
racism, poverty, and war as having a common denominator in
violence. Her indictment of the violence of poverty rose to
an eloquence not heard often in the campaign:

"Poverty can produce a most deadly kind of violence. In
this society violence against poor people and minority groups
is routine. I remind you that starving a child is violence;
suppressing a culture is violence; neglecting schoolchildren
is violence; punishing a mother and her child is violence;
discrimination against a workingman is violence; ghetto
housing is violence; ignoring medical needs is violence; contempt for equality is violence; even a lack of will power to
help humanity is a sick and sinister form of violence."

Turning to American involvement in Southeast Asia she
spoke as one mother to others in a forthright expression of
controlled rage that struck home with a force few had
equalled since her husband's death:

"Women must realize that the war in Vietman is the most
cruel and evil war in the history of mankind [applause], and
therefore it is our moral obligation to oppose it. If enough

women spoke out against the Vietnam war and stood firm
in their opposition even to being willing to go to jail if necessary, I think it would make a tremendous impact on the
President and the policymakers of this nation [applause].

"If we stop the war four months and one day sooner, we
could eliminate the need for the 10% surcharge tax. We
could create 400,000 new jobs with the money we could
save if we stopped the war... [a jet drowned out the remainder of the sentence]. If we stopped the war two months
sooner, we could build 300,000 new housing units with
the money. One hour of war could buy your community a
new school, hospital or cultural center. All of this is to say
that a guaranteed income, a job for those who need a job,
could be had if the war was stopped and the will created by
our government to act on behalf of its deprived citizens
[applause]."

To emphasize the importance of maintaining nonviolence
in the face of obstacles she quoted a poem, one that she was
to quote often that summer. Perhaps she liked it because
Dr. King had often used it as an admonition to his audiences.
This certainly added poignance to its repetition. She prefaced
it thus:

"The road to justice, peace and brotherhood is difficult. We
must renew our strength, increase our faith, and gird our
courage. In the words of the black poet, the late Langston
Hughes, a black mother counsels her son to keep faith in the
future. In her ungrammatical profundity she speaks:

> "Well, son, I'll tell you,
> Life for me ain't been no crystal stair.
> It's had tacks in it, and splinters,
>   and boards torn up,
> And places with no carpet on the floor,
>   bare.
> But all the time, I'se been a-
>   climbin' on

And reachin' landings and tur-
    nin' corners,
And sometimes goin' in the dark-
Where there ain't been no light.
So boy,
Don't you sit down on the step
'Cause you find it's kinda hard,
Don't you stop now;
'Cause I'se still goin', honey,
I'se still climbin',
And life for me, ain't been
    no crystal stair."

Then, inevitably, she concluded with an evocation of her husband's famous address on those same steps almost five years earlier, repeating the peroration of his "I Have a Dream" speech. The crowd was caught up in the words and the speaker: "'When we allow freedom to ring, when we let it ring from every village and every hamlet, from every state and every city, we will be able to speak of that day when *all* God's children — black men, white men, brown men, yellow men, red men; Jews and gentiles, Protestant and Catholic, will be able to join hands and sing in the old Negro spiritual, "Free at last —"'"

But now the crowd took up the chant, drowning her out: "'Free at last, thank God amighty I'm free at last!'" and everyone was on his feet in a tumultous standing ovation as Mrs. King left the microphone in tears.

Rev. Abernathy's address was next. It was supposed to be the culmination and acme of the day's speeches; but it was now approaching six o'clock, the hot sun hung right above the Memorial in everyone's eyes, the jets were still coming almost every minute; the crowd was dissipating ever faster; and after the emotional crescendo of Mrs. King's remarks, Abernathy could not help but sound anticlimatic. His opening statement confirmed this feeling:

"I do not pause this afternoon to tell you how delighted I am to have the privilege and the opportunity to stand before you and address you at this hour. I want you to know that I speak not only the words of Ralph David Abernathy, but I speak with a Divine Mandate from God, I speak with a mandate from the people, and I speak for the Poor People's Campaign assembled here in Washington D.C.; and in spite of the lateness of the hour and the confusion of this rostrum, I guarantee you that I will be heard."

The rest of the speech, however, if lengthy, was more articulate and carefully organized than any of his previous sermons during the summer. He reviewed the years since the earlier Washington march as the basis for the present grave national situation that made necessary this "all out, do-or-die effort to redeem the soul of America, lest she perish from the face of the earth." This, he insisted, "is what the Poor People's Campaign really is: it is a desperate effort to help America save itself."

Five times in the space of as many minutes he repeated the Campaign's determination to stay in Washington until real action was taken on its demands, in words like these: "Today, Solidarity Day, is not the end of the Poor People's Campaign. In fact, today is really only our beginning [applause]. We are only just beginning to fight. We will not give up the battle until the Congress of the United States decides to open the doors of America and allow the nation's poor to enter as full-fledged citizens into this land of wealth and opportunity."

Abernathy ticked off by department the results he believed the Campaign's focus on administrative agencies had achieved:

Agriculture: the "discovery" of $227 million the department was planning to return to the treasury (there was no assurance, however, that the funds would be spent or, if

spent, used for food); the introduction of federal food programs into more than 200 of the poorest counties now without
them; and a promise to increase the variety and nutritional
value of federally distributed surplus foods.

Office of Economic Opportunity: the "discovery" by the
office of an "extra" $25 million that was to be applied to
certain headstart, medical, and food programs in poor areas.

Health, Education and Welfare: pledges to simplify welfare application procedures, eliminate "man-in-the-house"
rules, and guarantee fair hearings for welfare clients whose
cases were closed; additional pledges of more specially trained
teachers to work in poverty areas, and the improvement of
health facilities in poor neighborhoods.

Department of Labor: pledges of jobs for 100,000 unem-
ployed workers by January 1969.

Housing and Urban Development: a pledge not to relocate
residents of urban renewal areas until suitable housing could
be arranged for them.

State Department: Abernathy asserted that Secretary of
State Dean Rusk had agreed to examine the land claims of
the Mexican-Americans in the Campaign and to coordinate
through the Agriculture Department United States food programs abroad with those at home so that hungry Americans
received from the government food equally as nutritious as
that given to hungry foreigners.

Justice Department: an agreement to take action against
the use of Mexican braceros as strikebreakers on large farms
in the Southwest and West.

Interior Department: a pledge to move faster in developing
school systems on reservations that would be controlled by
the Indians.

In each case Abernathy said the responses, while significant,
were not enough and vowed four more times to stay in the
capital until more acceptable responses were wrung from the

agencies. What an acceptable response would be he spelled
out in a six-point summary of Campaign demands:

1. An end to hunger
2. An end to bad housing
3. An end to unemployment and guaranteed incomes for
    those unable to work
4. Adequate health care for all citizens
5. Full equality of educational opportunity for all
6. An end to violence and repression at home and abroad
    (without specific mention of Vietnam).

These demands were far more than any administrative
action could achieve, and Abernathy went on to take Congress to task as a footdragging institution dominated by racist
Southern committee chairmen and to announce that the legislative branch was the Campaign's new target:

"These [chairmen] are the men who control our Congress,
and who stifle our nation's progress and against whom we
must mobilize our entire nation. There must be a national
outcry against leadership which refuses to act in the best
interests of all the people. And we must — and we will — stay
in Washington and fight until the nation rises up and our
demands are met."

He pledged to fight nonviolently; then — as if ten repeti-
tions weren't sufficient — told for the eleventh time of his determination to stay:

"I don't care — I said I don't care whether the Department
of Interior gives us a permit to stay in Resurrection City or
not [applause]. I-I-I received my permit a long time ago...
[jet noise]; I said I received my permit a long time ago. And
I received it in the form of no government; I received it
from no Constitution, but from God almighty [applause].
And I intend to stay here until justice rolls out of the halls
of Congress; and righteousness falls from the administration;
and the rough places of the agencies of government are made

plain; and the crooked deals with the military-industrial complex become straight; and the glory and abundance of God's
nation be revealed to the poor, and all races shall see it together [applause]."

Several black Baptist preachers were standing behind Abernathy, and as he built to a hoarse peroration their harsh, con-
trapuntal shouts came through between the phrases:

"I must leave you now, but as I leave you I want to leave
the words of an old Baptist hymn that always did my soul
good. Can I just say it to you this evening [shouts of "yeah!"
"Go ahead!" and jet noise]? It goes something like this:

> Beams of heaven as I go
> Through this wilderness below
> Guide my feet in peaceful ways ["Yeah"],
> Turn my midnights into days.
> When in the darkness I would grope,
> May I always see a star of hope
> And soon from all life's grief and pain,
> I shall be free, some day.
> Harder yet may be the fight ["Well!"]
> Right may often yield to might ["Lord have mercy!"].
> Wickedness awhile may reign,
> Satan's cause may seem to gain ["Yeah!"].
> But there is a God ["Yeah!"],
> There is a God ["Yeah! !"],
> There is a God ["Yeah! ! !"]
>   who rules aboves
> With a hand of power and a
>   heart of love ["Yeah!"].
> If I'm right he'll fight my battles,
> I shall be free, some day.
> I do not know
> I do not know ["Yeah!"],
> I do not know, how
>   long, t'will be ["Yeah!"],
> Or what the future holds for me ["Yeah!"]
> But this I know ["Yeah!"],
> This I know ["Yeah!"],

> *This* I *know [*"Yeah!!"*],*
> *If* Jesus *leads the way,*
> *I shall be free, some day." [Standing ovation]*

This was the end. Jesse Jackson and Hosea Williams read a Poor People's Litany and someone led the singing of "We Shall Overcome," but as soon as the applause for Abernathy had died down the remainder of the crowd was scattering across the littered grass, headed for home.

5

Violence Inside and Out

The ceremonies were over, but as night fell on Washington, SCLC was not yet finished with Solidarity Day. The last really heavy rain had fallen the 12th and 13th, the beginning of the Agriculture vigil; and by the weekend before the big rally, the camp was drying out and again roiling with violence. The outbreaks seemed more intense now, with beatings and robberies occurring almost hourly. The local press was no doubt pleased to report these outbreaks in detail; but the accounts, it must be said, were not exaggerated very much. Resurrection City in its final week was unquestionably a turbulent and dangerous place. Within the city, the disturbances were a prime object of staff and resident attention, but nothing anyone did was able to stem the tide.

About 9:30 Wednesday night, after the site had been turned into mud once again by a brief but heavy rain, 60 residents left to join Dr. King's brother, Rev. A. D. Williams King, at the Statler-Hilton Hotel, where he and several other staff had been refused service because their attire — denim workclothes — was not considered appropriate. King told the management he would bring campaigners from the City to demonstrate at the hotel if his group was not served. At the sight of busloads of supporters the management relented, called police to keep watch on the situation, and served the whole group expensive steak dinners. They also made no public complaints when, after a conference, the campaigners paid only $198 of the $495 bill.

Returning to the campsite around 1:00 A.M., some of the diners began taunting policemen on duty at the park's western edge. They were joined by others who were angry over rumors spreading through the camp that a resident hit with a baseball bat the night before had died and that another camper had been stabbed by a cop. The rumors were finally proved false; the young man referred to had sustained a skull fracture when he and 20 other young campaigners broke up a softball game near the campsite Tuesday evening. He had just regained consciousness at George Washington University Hospital and was in no danger. The stabbing in the other rumor also took place, but inside Resurrection City and thus it was unlikely a policeman was the assailant.

The police responded by forcing them back toward the main gate. Bottles and canned food flew out of the retreating crowd at the officers, and the gathering continued to grow in size and hostility. Police reinforcements arrived, some of them armed with shotguns. Several cooler-headed marshals asked the police to move back to reduce the tension and allow them to maneuver the milling, shouting crowd back into the campsite; but only when Andrew Young, Hosea Williams, and James Bevel arrived at 1:45 did the people begin returning to their shanties. Bevel asked the police to move back to the parking lot on the edge of the park, telling them, "When you get immature bottle-throwers together with immature policemen you have the makings of a riot." The police moved back, the shotguns were put away, and the camp was quiet for the remaining few hours of darkness.

Now that Solidarity Day was at last behind him, Rev. Abernathy was ready to step up the tempo of demonstrations. He told a press conference Thursday afternoon, "We wanted to move the Congress and the federal agencies we visited ... by going step by step to show what could be done. Now it's apparent they are not going to respond. I think it's just a racist Congress." Because of the unsatisfactory response, he said, the Campaign would have to "escalate" its actions. Staff members were saying off the record that Monday, June 24, was the date mass arrests would begin. Similar declarations had been made weekly since the Campaign settled in Washington; but staff members were now admitting privately to newsmen that arrests had been deliberately avoided previously for fear of limiting Solidarity Day's success, and so the anouncement was taken seriously.

At the same hour Abernathy was threatening escalation, a hundred campaigners were approaching the Agriculture Department to do some premature escalating of their own. None of the top staff except Hosea Williams was present, and Williams left soon after the group arrived. After pausing to eat hot lunches delivered by a catering truck, the second echelon staff members leading the group demanded to see Agriculture Secretary Orville Freeman. They were first told the Secretary was busy, and later that he would meet with not more than 12 of the demonstrators. This was not satisfactory to the staff, and they began marching around the building, dropping off small groups at each entrance until all the doorways were filled and blocked. Assistant Secretary Joseph M. Robertson, who was representing Freeman, conferred briefly with another Department executive, then asked police to clear the doorways, and arrests began.

The police were quiet and methodical at first. They utilized a special mass arrest procedure in which an arrest team in a single operation picked up and searched a demonstrator, filled out the necessary papers and attached to them an instant mugshot snapped with a Polaroid Swinger. The fully processed "arrestee" was then deposited in a bus for transportation to jail. As the arrest team proceeded from one door to the next, it was preceded by a private attorney, Frank Reeves, who was the head of SCLC's volunteer legal assistance group. Reeves obviously felt the sit-in was not part of Campaign strategy, and told the demonstrators so, warning them as well that the official policy was "jail — no bail" and the penalties for their action could be 90-day sentences and $250 fines. But the sit-ins were adamant, even defiant. They had waited long enough for some action.

At 6:00 P.M., when about 50 persons had been arrested, police radios brought news that a second contingent of marchers was forming in Resurrection City and would be heading for the Agriculture complex shortly. The main doorways of the building had been cleared, and Assistant Secretary Robertson said he was going to tell Department employees blocked inside the building by the sit-in to leave through them. Police sent the busses of prisoners off to men's and women's jails, and it seemed that with the building opened up, no more arrests were to be made.

A few moments later a third-echelon SCLC organizer named Leon Hall appeared on the scene with several dozen more marchers, and walked around the building, ordering the demonstrators still blocking doors to get up and follow him, which they did. When he came upon Attorney Reeves advising a group of sit-ins, he interrupted him harshly: "Don't listen to him, he works for Freeman.... You are not running our demonstration."

Hall continued: "Your job is to get us out of jail, not to worry how we get in. You ain't helping us, you are helping them. You are a white man's nigger."

Reeves turned angrily back to the campaigners in the doorway. Hall and his crowd of 50 walked on to the southeast corner of the building, the intersection of Independence Avenue and 12th Street, and began blocking traffic on both streets.

Traffic, well into Washington's frantic evening rush hour,

backed up, honking, immediately. The police in the area were at first caught off guard and confused by the blockade. Then an officer came up and told his men to clear the intersection, but to be gentle about it. As the police advanced across 12th Street the demonstrators retreated to the corner, then blocked Independence Avenue. When the police advanced on them there, they returned to 12th Street.

The "mobile" tactics were all several policemen needed. One was overheard saying, "I've been waiting for this for a long time," as he jammed his billy club across a marcher's neck and dragged him by the head to the curb. A young man on crutches with hippie-length hair, caught in a rush of marchers running from the sudden flailing of nightsticks, could not get out of the police's path: four officers grabbed him, lifted him to the sidewalk, and beat him. He crumpled to the ground, and while he was falling, an officer grabbed one crutch and without looking flung it over his shoulder. The crutch skidded across the asphalt and slammed into the opposite curb.

Demonstrators, fleeing the clubs, headed around the Agriculture Building towards 14th Street. Once there, they again blocked traffic, with the police not far behind. The lieutenants repeated — and the men again ignored — instructions to control themselves. One grinning sergeant grabbed a black man, split his scalp wide open and knocked him unconscious with a single smashing blow that was heard over a block away. A 68-year-old white lady campaigner from Georgia fell across a young man being clubbed to protect him; for her trouble she also was beaten and then carried away, like a corpse, one policeman on each limb. Her son, who is blind and deaf, was likewise pounded. Several policemen actually went berserk and had to be held back by other officers.

The assaults and sit-ins continued for half an hour. Then the remaining marchers, enraged by the police assaults, gathered on a corner trading curses and taunts with their adversaries. Leon Hall, who had not been arrested, urged them to go back into the street. Several people disagreed with him, and while they argued, Attorney Reeves ran up to the group and shouted for them to come to the north side of the building because Rev. Abernathy wanted to speak to them.

As they straggled around to the main entrance, the marchers were cheered to see 150 of their comrades marching from the camp to join them. Hosea Williams and Jesse Jackson had now arrived, and they spoke to the crowd while other staff members circulated through and kept it under control. "This is not the first time poor folks has had to bleed for this country," Williams shouted, "and it won't be the last. We got the makings of a movement. Solidarity Day gave it to us." He said that Abernathy had wanted to meet them, but they had told him to stay at the meeting he was in to plan further strategy. "Tomorrow afternoon," Williams told them, "he is gonna lead himself and give them a chance to beat his head." The crowd cheered.

Jesse Jackson urged them to keep order: "We must not become a mob. We must remain a movement. Now that the warfare is on, shape up or ship out. Those of you who cannot undertake the discipline of nonviolence, you do not have the courage of a man to place your body on the line for what you believe. We saw the people who were good soldiers. They were the ones who stayed when the rains came. It was the rains that separated the weak from the strong. I'm tired of marching and tired of talking, but I have no fear of the river of blood."

They told the group to follow them back to Resurrection City, where they would eat, bind their wounds, and prepare for Friday's action. The lines, nearly 500 strong now, crossed 14th Street and filed past the Washington Monument toward the camp, many of them taunting the escorting police as they went.

At 17th Street, which divides the Washington Monument

grounds from West Potomac Park, a single policeman was on duty; he stopped traffic so the marchers could pass. After several dozen had crossed, a few suddenly lay down in the street or turned to start arguing with drivers in the nearest cars. Campaign marshals rushed in and pleaded with them to leave the street and go into the camp. The street cleared enough so a few cars could pass, then the officer signaled for traffic to stop again. A white woman in a red Bonneville northbound obediently put on her brakes; but when she saw several angry black men in the street heading for her car, she panicked, and sent the Bonneville screaming through the crowd, marchers diving out of its path and spinning off its headlights. Bottles and rocks flew after the car, bouncing off its sides for several dozen yards. Southbound drivers who saw her racing past also panicked, banging into each other and going over the curb to turn around and get out of the area. Their anger rekindled, marchers began coming back toward 17th Street from Resurrection City.

Police reinforcements began arriving about this time, to clear the street with much the same techniques they had employed earlier. For the next hour the area teetered on the brink of a riot. The sight of uniforms inflamed the people, and within thirty minutes 200 policemen were sealing off the entire eastern end of the park. Only several Campaign marshals, in what was probably their finest hour, prevented a more serious outbreak. A steady hail of rocks, bricks, and bottles was aimed at the nearest policemen, who stayed just out of range and seemed to enjoy dancing about and dodging them. Dozens of men, some drunk, others blind with rage, tried to charge the heavily armed police lines with bricks, beer can openers or their bare fists; the marshals ran back and forth tackling them, slapping their faces when they were down to bring them to their senses. The scrimmage kept up until the police tired of the game and began throwing tear gas canisters, at least 40 of them, into the crowd.

The clouds of gas drove the marchers back behind the fence, but it did not calm them down.

A little while later, a town meeting was held in the camp, but calls for violent retaliation almost broke it up. One man cried: "The Indians want to fight to get their land back. The Mexican-Americans say they'll fight. Everybody can fight except the black people. Why?" Another speaker demanded a Black Power meeting be held the next day to plan some new and more militant response to the police actions. Another called for a night march to leave Resurrection City right then and to head for 14th and U Streets, the heart of Washington's ghetto, where, he said, they would be joined by "demonstrators who'll really demonstrate." The call was relayed to the several hundred police now ringing the camp, who broke out gas masks, replenished supplies of grenades, readied a 10,000 watt spotlight and sealed off the street approaching the camp. But the SCLC staff members who were on hand had been through all this before, and they mounted a strong polemical counterattack against those talking about violence. James Bevel summed up their case in a slashing, heated sermon:

"There are a lot of people, a lot of fighting brothers, who want to play radical games and throw a rock at a policeman with a tommy gun. The question of violence and nonviolence is not at stake, the question of wisdom or foolishness is at stake.

"A lot of folks say, 'We're going to go out here and fight a lot of honkie cops,' trying to play on the emotionalism of people. What is your strategy for breaking out of an economic trap? That's the question. What is your strategy for putting money into the ghetto schools? What is your strategy for taking over the black community and owning the stores in those communities? What is your strategy for that?

"Now . . . let me push on up since I'm a revolutionary and don't mind discussing it. I will discuss it with brothers in public. . . . Running past a power plant and burning down a pawn shop does not constitute a revolution. Burning down a liquor store does not constitute a revolution. . . . If you were going to use violence as a tool, you would kill strategic people in order to create fear. In other words, when racist legislators can walk around without fear of their lives, ain't no black cat serious about violent revolution. When Congressman X can walk down the street drunk and mess up black children every day, ain't no black boy serious about revolution. When the judges in Chicago who sent up 200,-000 black children to jail are safe, and across the street black cats are drinking wine and black cats are talking crap, they wasn't serious about violent revolution. I know violence. I studied violence. You use violence in order to set up a certain syndrome in people and when a guy walking around with a tomahawk argues with an atomic bomb, he's not serious."

It was a powerful rebuke of the immature "guerilla" mentality. But it was not entirely clear whether Bevel's antagonists were adolescent "guerillas" talking romantic nonsense about revolution with guns, or just toughs from the ghetto streets to whom violence was not a rationalized program but simply a fact of their lives, a reflex. The sermon was almost irrelevant in any case because the really dangerous people in the camp weren't listening. They were out in the darkness going about their business — drinking, stealing, fighting, baiting police. It was Rev. Abernathy who quieted the camp, by ignoring the call for a night march, coaxing the women into their shanties and diverting the men into security duties. He told them to make "a sweep through the city for any CIA men who might be planted with Molotov cocktails," and promised nervous residents he would keep the police from coming inside the fence. "Women," he pleaded, "go back to your huts. Men, let us stand watch. We need some men to survey this camp. There are some men who want to do some bad business tonight.

... Women, go to sleep... we're not going to have any trouble tonight because I'm going to be in control of these streets... go to bed... I want you all to go to bed... I want you all to go to bed... if police come in here tonight it'll be over me... Madam, won't you go to your shack? Isn't that wonderful...?"

The Campaign suffered other setbacks Thursday besides the aftermath of the 86 arrests at the Agriculture Department. On Capitol Hill influential members of both houses were making it plain that their patience with the encampment was exhausted. House Rules Committee Chairman William Colmer of Mississippi stated in response to questions that the Cramer bill would be called up for a vote the next week if the Campaign had not vacated the campsite by then. And Senator Robert Byrd, who had earlier agreed to the week's extension of the park permit, announced he would not consider any further extensions. "The Executive Department," he said, "ought to get those people out of there, even if they have to be carried out."

That afternoon, the *Washington Daily News* was interviewing Alvin Jackson, a black electrician who had been the deputy chief marshal at Resurrection City. Jackson resigned Thursday, heartbroken, he said, because violence was destroying the City. "This is a great campaign and a just one," he said, "and it has just goals." But "the reason the population of this city is going down is not mud, poor food, rain or lousy homes... the reason they leave is that men are getting tired of coming home from a day's picketing to find their belongings stolen or their wife raped.... There are rapes, robberies, and cuttings every day, and there is nothing we can do about it even when we catch the guys who did it. If the leaders there don't do something soon this is going to be known as blood city instead of Resurrection City." The police estimate of 100 violent incidents in the City's month of existence he called "very conservative."

As soon as the story came out, SCLC officials were denying
that Jackson ever had anything to do with the security force,
and rumors were soon spread that he was probably planted by
the Administration for the sole purpose of discrediting the
Campaign in just such a dramatic fashion. The latter charge
was never substantiated, and there was in fact frustration
aplenty in West Potomac Park for any serious-minded person.

Ralph Abernathy must have gone to bed early Friday
morning discouraged and sick at heart — if indeed he went to
bed at all. The rush of events gave him little time to rest:
not long after sunrise Friday, he was called to an unscheduled
meeting at Hawthorne School with the angry Mexican-
American leaders. The topics of discussion at the meeting
were kept confidential, but it amounted to a requiem for
the Campaign's multiethnic coalition. Reies Tijerina and the
other Hispanic leader, Corky Gonzalez, were by now almost completely disenchanted with SCLC leadership; they
were already quietly sending their people home, in twos
and threes to avoid publicity. Reporters had noticed when
40 of Tijerina's group left Washington for New Mexico
on Thursday. Tijerina affably explained that the bus had
been chartered and paid for a round trip before they came to
Washington and they would not get a refund if it was not
used. The passengers would soon be replaced by new recruits, he promised; but the recruits never came, and it is
unlikely Tijerina requested any. Some of the trouble from
Resurrection City had been seeping into Hawthorne's relatively well-disciplined halls, exacerbating the intergroup hostility. And it is known that Tijerina and Gonzalez were
skeptical of the entire SCLC demonstration and mass arrest
strategy. Frequent calls had gone out to Hawthorne for troops
to join and enlarge demonstrations, and most of them had
been ignored. The Mexican-American leaders were reportedly
very upset by Thursday's Agriculture confrontation; they felt

the beatings of old men and women were needlessly pro-
voked and showed a lack of concern by the SCLC leaders
for their followers. Friday's meeting was undoubtedly the
showdown.

Hints of the meeting's atmosphere leaked out almost inadvertently at a noontime press conference held on the
school's front steps. Most of the reporters clustered around
the leaders did not seem aware that anything unusual was
afoot, and most questions were routine and unprobing.

"We invited Dr. Abernathy," Corky Gonzalez began, "because we were concerned with what the activities and the
new plans for the future would be for the Poor People's
Campaign. We sat down to discuss this and to initiate and
continue with the National Steering Committee which will
make decisions and policy and determine the policy and the
strategy of the Poor People's Campaign."

"We've had a most fruitful discussion," Abernathy allowed. He said the Steering Committee's decisions for future
plans would be announced Saturday morning following a
meeting that evening, adding, "there was one decision
reached that I should announce to you, and that is the fact
that we agreed that in the days now following Solidarity Day
we will remain united and we will move forward as poor
Mexican-Americans, poor whites from Appalachia, American
Indians, poor Puerto Ricans and poor blacks, and we're going
to stand as one united front together. If we go up, we go up
together and if we go down, we all will go down together."

Microphones were aimed at Tijerina: "Do you support
demonstrations like the one last night?"

Tijerina paused. "We didn't demonstrate last night," he
said.

"Well, do you support that kind of demonstration?"

"Well...Rev. Abernathy has said those things will be
discussed at this afternoon's Steering Committee Meeting."

"Mr. Tijerina, is there any further word on whether the Mexican-Americans will move into Resurrection City?"

"That will be discussed also."

A lady reporter: "Rev. Abernathy, was your meeting harmonious this — "

"It was as harmonious," he interrupted, throwing one arm around Tijerina and the other around Gonzalez, "as we are ... standing together now. We are all together. . . . That's the type of unity that we have and that's the type of unity that we're going to maintain now that Solidarity Day is behind us." The others smiled weakly and said nothing.

One reporter was a little suspicious: "What differences were there that prompted you to have this meeting?"

Abernathy dodged: "I came at the invitation of several leaders of various groups here participating in the Poor People's Campaign because we have come to a new phase in the movement with the completion of Solidarity Day." The reporter did not pursue the matter, and Abernathy declined other questions, indicating he would deal with them at another press conference at 2:30 that afternoon.

At the later conference, held by the Reflecting Pool outside Resurrection City's gates, Abernathy haltingly read a long statement that he had apparently not seen before. It rebuked the police beatings and use of tear gas the evening before, then admitted there had been violence within Resurrection City as well: "These incidents are few, admittedly, but they are nevertheless very unfortunate. Some of them, I am sure, are caused by infiltrators, paid infiltrators. Residents of Resurrection City, including marshals and SCLC staff members, have reported to me that some people have entered the campsite to make trouble. We do try to maintain tight security in the city, but we have never been able to keep out all enemies from a movement which is essentially free and open. . . . The streets of Resurrection City are not the shady boulevards of

Bethesda and Chevy Chase, but the broiling pavements of Watts and the unpaved lanes of Mississippi where poor people have always been locked up by America. And also in Resurrection City you will find, America, the fruit of your evil.... I make no excuse for violence, here or anywhere. It is wrong.... I do not want the poor people to imitate the lowest form of behavior in a racist society.... But there is a greater evil than a few outbreaks in Resurrection City. It is the evil of widespread poverty in America, and I challenge America, I challenge the press...and every leader in the power structure which inflicts poverty on millions of Americans to tell me what their excuse is for poverty.... I am saying to America, you can blame me for violence in Resurrection City if you wish; I accept it. But who is to blame for the violence of slums, the violence of discrimination, the violence of broken promises and lies to the poor, the violence of unequal and inadequate education, the violence of a punitive welfare system, the violence of cheating American Indians and Mexican-Americans and Appalachian whites and northern and southern blacks?"

In an almost desperate effort to turn the criticism back on itself, Abernathy summed up his challenge in one question which he said symbolized all the issues he was raising and to which he demanded a public answer from the President: "The question is: why does the United States government pay the Mississippi plantation of a United States Senator more than $13,000 a month not to grow food or fibre, and at the same time why does the government pay a starving child... [jet noise forced him to pause] in Mississippi only $9 a month, and what are you going to do about it?" He repeated the question, and said, "If the President, speaking for this society, has the courage to answer this question directly, then maybe America can find the courage to deal with all the problems suggested by this question. If not, God help this sick nation." He called for all supporters of the Campaign to besiege the President and Congress with letters, telegrams and telephone calls demanding an answer.

The statement was eloquent, but the reporters showed little interest in it. After asking which Senator he was referring to [Democrat James O. Eastland, Chairman of the Senate Judiciary Committee], the questions centered on the reports of paid infiltrators and the matter of Resurrection City's permit, which was to expire two days later. He declined to give any details about the alleged infiltrators (staff members later admitted privately that they had no evidence of deliberate infiltration). Asked if he intended to stay in the Park past the deadline if the permit was not renewed, he replied that he did indeed plan to stay. Other newsmen asked him the same question two or three more times, as if they didn't believe their ears; Abernathy patiently repeated himself. Asked why he wasn't leading a demonstration this afternoon, he admitted that "organizational problems" leading to the unexpected Hawthorne meeting had forced him to change plans, but promised that a march would leave the campsite for the Agriculture Department before the day was over.

The press conference began an hour late, and the delay probably changed the outcome of the afternoon's march. Soon after the conference broke up, the camp's PA system came alive, with Hosea Williams's voice calling for marchers to assemble. Only those who were ready to go to jail should come, he warned. Twenty minutes later a long file left the camp, headed east towards the Agriculture complex.

At the target building, the police had been ready for over an hour with paddy wagons, arrest teams, and 100 men waiting near the main driveway. When a Campaign first-aid team arrived with stretchers and bandages, the scene seemed set for a rerun of Thursday's confrontation, conducted this time with more discipline.

But when the marchers' ranks became visible at the crest of the Washington Monument's hill, it was 5:15 P.M., and

the Department's employees were almost all out of the building. The group, led by Jesse Jackson, circled the building
singing and clapping, dropping off marchers at each door.
As they received their assignments, the demonstrators —
many of them teenagers — flopped down and linked arms,
looking grim but determined, and ready for the worst. By
the time all the entrances were blocked, and the police
had not made any move to start arrests, it began to dawn on
them that they weren't really obstructing anything. Agricul-
ure officials said as much, indicating that since the entrances
were not being used, they had no plans to ask the police for
arrests. After an impromptu whispered conference with other
staff members, Jackson announced that the demonstrators
would stay all weekend and confront the police when employees tried to enter the blockaded entrances Monday morning. The marchers, when given these new instructions, obediently started bedding down in the doorways for the night.

Back at the campsite, a young man named Johnny Patterson was being arrested by police for armed robbery. Mr.
Patterson's arrest was almost as embarrassing to the harassed
Campaign leadership as the resignation of Alvin Jackson,
because Patterson was the leader of a senior group of marshals
who called themselves Tent City Rangers. The Rangers had
their own distinctive uniforms of white denims, special metal
badges, and Australian bush hats, and most were older than
the other marshals. The group had earned a reputation both
with the press and the SCLC staff as the coolest and most
dependable members of the encampment's volatile security
forces. The loss of one of their few good men on such a
charge the day after Alvin Jackson's resignation was doubly
unfortunate; and the word around the camp among "informed
sources" was that the charges were not simply harassment,
that Patterson may well have pulled a few stickups to help
finance his Rangers' activities.

Another piece of bad news was the Interior Department's decision, leaked to the press in late afternoon, to refuse any further extensions of Resurrection City's permit. SCLC had been negotiating with federal officials all week for an extension. Now, responding to Congressional pressure and widespread negative reaction to the aftermath of Thursday's demonstration, the Administration had made its move. Probably the Administration felt the Campaign was now sufficiently discredited that the camp could be closed by force if necessary without stirring much reaction in the nation's ghettos. Abernathy earlier had warned of nationwide riots if his campers were turned out. The camp's mimeographed newspaper, *True Unity News,* in its issue of June 21 also took up the cry: "Ghetto leaders from across the nation warn that Resurrection City is not to be evicted. The grapevine reports that if such an attempt is made, mass rioting will be the result.

"One of the spokesmen, who declined the use of his name, declared that such action would create conditions that would make the aftermath of Dr. King's slaying mere child's play, and would evoke violence without comparison in American history."

These threats might have intimidated someone in May, but they made little impression now.

Friday night a Campaign mass meeting was held at St. Stephen's Baptist Church, where the church was full and the crowd unusually boisterous. The featured preacher of the evening was Rev. C. L. Franklin of Detroit. Rev. Franklin is the father of Miss Aretha Franklin, a very successful soul singer, and he was an old friend of Dr. King. A solidly built man with sleek shiny hair and a booming voice, Rev. Franklin was a real master of the black Baptist preacher's art; he enjoyed his work, and the crowd enjoyed him. His sermon was free-form development of the theme, "They Wouldn't

Bow," from the Bible account of Shadrach, Meshach and Abednego, who were placed in a fiery furnace for their refusal to worship the pagan gods of Babylon.

"I hope I can get somebody to pray with me tonight," he began, warming them up, "because you know, I'm a *Negro* preacher, and I like to talk to people and have people talk *back* to me." He paused while they roared their pleasure. "I want to talk to you tonight about 'They Wouldn't Bow.'

"Now we *know* that the God whom we serve is able to de*liv*er us. But if He chooses *not* — if his Providence dictates that we must *suffer,* we still will not bow." He pointed at a girl dozing in the third row. "Now shake her right there so she can hear my sermon," he said, chuckling. "I want her to stay awake at *least* til I get started. . . . Basically," he went on, "I'm from Main. I don't mean the state of Maine, I mean the main part of Mississippi." The people roared again, recognizing a fine performer when they heard one.

He led them through a summary of Babylon's victory over Judah and the captivity that followed. "And Nebudchadnez-zor, in order to insure his reign ["Yeah!"] raped as it were the country of Judah. ["Well!"] They took away her soldiers; they took away her businessmen ["Yeah!"]; they took away her scholars; they took away even — her leadership of *re-ligious* thought. ["Well!"] . . . And of course they placed them in a ghetto in Babylon. And — the Psalmist pictured it rather graphically, he said their situation was so *aw*ful that they felt like a composite *n*ational body ["Yeah!"] that had died: that its very skin, its sinew, its flesh had deteriorated ["Yeah!"] leaving only a national skeleton ["HmHm"]; and that their hearts had lost their song ["All right!"]; the choir members left the *choir* ["Yeah!"] and the musicians hung up their harps on the willow ["Well, well well!"], and they refused to sing ["Yeah!"]. And — uh — so that not *only* was there *sad*ness and *hope*-less-ness, depravity or frustration

["Well!"], there was — for them — *death*.... Are you praying?" ["Yeah!"]

Shadrach, Meshach and Abednego, who were prominent
in the Babylonian king's service, were turned in by spies for
not bowing to the local gods: "So the spies reported to the
king, 'These native *Jews,* they did not recognize the *law!'*
But you know, there are *higher* laws ["Preach Sir!" "Come
on!"]. There are *higher* laws. There are laws and there are
loyalties ["Yeah!"] *above* patriotic laws ["Break it up!"], and
that loyalty is to *God.*" ["Yeah!"]

He peered down at his audience: *"You* don't *hear* what
I'm sayin'." [Laughter.]

The three were arrested and called before the king, who
had been their benefactor and thought the matter was a misunderstanding. He tried to clear it up by asking them to make
the ritual motions for him at a signal. "But they said, 'King,
we're not gon' bow. ["All right!"] We didn't misunderstand.
We knew what the law was. ["Well!"] It wasn't a mistake,
it was a de*libe*rate thing. ["Yeah!"] We understood it *thor-
oughly.* ["Yeah!"] We didn't in*tend to bow!* [Cheers and
applause.] So there's no *need* of *wast*ing any time goin' back
over this whole thing ["Yeah!"], 'cause if you go back over
it and we hear it, we're *still* not gon' bow [Cheers and applause.]

...And of *course,* they were taken to a fiery furnace —
you don't hear me. *["Yeah!"* "Come on!"] Somebody said
the other day that our re*pub*lic is making the mis*take* of putting *law* above *justice* — *you* don't hear me. ["Come on!"] I
feel like if the state was as concerned about *justice* as they
are about law and *order* ["Come on now!"] — there wouldn't
be any *need* for Resurrection City. [Applause.]

"But they wouldn't bow...and of *course* ...they were led
down to a fiery *furnace.* ... And of *course,* the power structure *will* put you in jail ["Yeah!"]; they *will* take you to the
electric chair ["Yessir!" "Take your time!"]; they *will* shoot

you down — or have you shot down ["Yessir!" "That's right!"]; they will subject you to indignities and humiliations ["Come on!"], and reduce you to poverty circum*stances*. ["Yeah!"] But *I* think, all of us should make one *firm* resolution today: *we're not gon' bow!* [Extended applause.]

"Now God has a way of de*li*verance. ["Oh Lord!"] In this particular case, He beat those young men to the furnace ["Yes He did!"] — *you* don't *hear* me. But — if you *must* face the *jails* ["If you must!"]; if you *must* face the *mob* ["Oh yeah!"]; if you must face ["If you must!"] the *dogs;* if you must *face* the gallopin' horses ["Yeah!"], you oughta make up in your *mind,* you're not gonna bow!" [Cheers and applause.]

At this point Franklin's delivery crossed the line between speaking and singing as he rose towards a crescendo, and the responses from the crowd became tumultuous and almost continuous, beyond hope of reproduction in print. The roots of his famous daughter's vocal style could be heard reverberating in his voice. At the climax, he suddenly turned and sat down, leaving the crowd in mid-cheer. But it was only a flourish; he was on his feet again in a few seconds, shouting and singing to them and with them, finally leading the church in the hymn, "I'm Gonna Trust in the Lord Until I Die," and then sitting down exhausted, dramatically wiping his streaming face with a large white handkerchief.

It was a magnificent performance, unequalled during the Campaign in brilliance of delivery or frenzy of response. It was the closest the Washington mass meetings ever came to the kind of exultation that makes a movement the center of a community's attention the way it was in Selma.

Jesse Jackson followed Franklin, and showed he was no mean preacher himself:

"*This* night — *this* night, we have about 200 people at the Agriculture Department.... Now they said that you have come *late* for the workers who have gotten off Friday. But what they didn't know is that we are very *early* for the ones comin' on *Monday*. [Applause.] Tonight, tomorrow night and Sunday, we are taking over door by door; if we can't live at Resurrection City, we would rather be at the Agriculture Department *any*way. [Laughter and applause.]

"Resurrection City is a *tem*porary state. I mean, you don't just keep *wall*owin' in the Resurrection — once the Resurrection is *est*ablished, then you 'go ye into all the *world*.' Now we have *had* a Resurrection; it is now time to go *ye* into the world and *stop* ye at the Agriculture Department. [Laughter and applause.]

"At the *A*griculture De*part*ment — *early* Monday mornin', we are *goin'* to *see* ["Amen"], are the jails *high* enough ["All *right!*"], are the rivers *deep* enough ["Come on now!"], to *hold* back the kinda freedom I wanna see Monday mornin' — *y'all hear me Negroes?* ["Yeah! We hear ya!"] . . . This is important now, because we're talkin' about goin' to *jail* — we're talkin' about jail with no bail, we ain't talkin' about goin' in there to pay our way out Monday. . . . The women that have come here know what's at stake — they're stronger than most of us. Don't you men start talkin' about 'well, those police, they whippin', they broke some girl's arm, and-uh we gon' fight them for the women' — *no!* Don't you fight them *for* the women: you pro*tect* the *wo*men and express your manhood by your willingness to *suf*fer, not by your ability to cuss.

"Now I just wanta set the record very straight — and if you cannot *make* it, *shake* it! [Scattered applause.] No no, I'm quite serious. . . . If I am standing there . . . when you see my *blood,* do not allow the blood to drive your feet to kick, but let my blood drive your intellect to *think* . . . some of us *must* bleed in order that others might live; but we've made that decision. So don't start tryin' to fight somebody for me. I can take care of me [scattered applause] — no, don't clap, I want you to hear that very well."

The church applauded Jackson enthusiastically, but when the rally was over few of them joined the marchers at Agriculture, who spent the night huddled in their unused doorways. At Resurrection City, an outbreak seemed near when a rumor swept the camp about 2:00 A.M. that Stokely Carmichael had been shot. About 150 angry young people gathered at the gate shouting at police, who said they would check out the report, called for reinforcements nervously, and began donning their riot equipment. Calm was restored when Rev. Abernathy came on the camp PA system: "Someone in this camp is trying to start trouble. Stokely Carmichael has not been shot. We have verified this." The sullen crowd slowly dispersed.

Neither Abernathy nor any Mexican-Americans appeared at Friday's mass meeting; they were at the Methodist Building in a summit conference that lasted well after midnight. They evidently did not come to any firm agreements, because at his Saturday press conference Abernathy put off until Monday the promised details of the Campaign's "new phase." Surprisingly, he called off the Agriculture vigil, in order to concentrate, he said, on two days of spiritual rededication, housecleaning, and screening of the residents in preparation for the "long, difficult work of the Campaign." There were reports that the Mexican-Americans had demanded the vigil be called off because it had not been authorized by the full multi-ethnic Steering Committee.

Reies Tijerina was present at the conference, and Abernathy was asked if his followers were now preparing to move into the camp. He answered vaguely that "plans call for all of the people to move into the city." Tijerina also hedged, saying only, "We're supporting the words of Rev. Abernathy."

The camp's permit, which had only a few more than 24 hours yet to run, was the major concern of reporters at the conference. Abernathy responded to their questions by stag-

ing a ceremony in which a feather-bedecked Indian, identi-
fied as George Crow Flies High, chief of the Hidasta tribe,
presented him with a "proclamation of temporary cession,"
in the name of the land's original Indian owners, allowing
him to stay on the Park land as long as he wanted to stay.
Abernathy then called for a National Day of Prayer on
Sunday: "We ask that people of good will everywhere pray
for the purification of our nation, for a rededication to nonviolence, for an end to hunger and for the preservation of
Resurrection City, the symbol of the Campaign."

The leadership's screening, like previous announced re-
organizations and purifications, did not amount to much.
Most of the top staff disappeared into strategy sessions except
for the few who conducted a late evening rally; assaults and
robberies continued unabated in the Park area, and about
12:30 A.M., Sunday morning, the camp's luck finally ran out.

Police lobbed more than 75 tear gas grenades into the
southwest corner of the darkened campsite. The gas billowed
east on a slight breeze, quickly engulfing the entire shantytown. After the first round of grenades were thrown, Andrew
Young approached police lines, pleading with them to stop.
He was threatened with arrest, and the canisters continued
arching over the fence. Residents, most of them women and
children in nightclothes, were routed from their cots and
fled coughing and screaming along the Reflecting Pool, across
17th Street and up the hill to the brightly lit Washington
Monument. There they collected themselves, bathed burning eyes in water fountains, and talked to each other about
what had happened. They were a pathetic and moving sight,
these people, most of them black, silhouetted in the glare of
huge spotlights and looking tiredly down on the White
House and gray government buildings visible in the distance
behind their own lights. After collecting themselves, and
when the gas seemed to be dissipating, they began trickling
back down through the darkness to their homes.

Several people were injured in the attack, overcome by gas and trampled as they lay gasping in the rutted, half-dried pathways. Accounts of how the barrage started conflicted wildly: the police said it was purely a response to repeated incidents during the evening in which bottles, bricks, and flaming sticks were thrown at them and at passing cars. Some campers swore they saw policemen smashing bottles along Independence Avenue earlier in the evening, planting evidence for their claim. It is known that rocks and bottles were thrown at police after the tear gas barrage began. But it is hard to imagine provocations short of outright assaults that would have required a response of that magnitude; the police were obviously enjoying their work.

Several dozen residents gathered in the City's culture tent after their return from the Washington Monument. James Bevel and Jesse Jackson spoke to them. Jackson said again that screening was necessary if the Campaign was to confront the government in the proper nonviolent fashion. He added that while the leadership would have to tell the press the barrage had been the police's fault, that he and the residents both knew there were young people — "Jitterbugs" he called them — who had been provoking the police. Bevel lectured them on the complexities of running a social movement. He said leadership of social movements was a science and a profession like medicine, and that the relationship of the leadership to a movement was like that of a doctor to his patient or an airline pilot to his passengers. He also compared a movement to a chess game in which each side made moves, and admitted that SCLC had made several bad moves, and that this had much to do with the Campaign's beleagured situation. But he expressed confidence that the professionals in the SCLC leadership would be able to analyze the situation correctly and plan new moves to overcome their errors. It was surprising to hear these two making such admissions to that large a group, even without newsmen around.

The meeting did not last long. Bevel announced that a workshop would be held at 3:00 P.M. Sunday afternoon, at which residents would learn the plans for action when the permit expired. With a heavy security watch posted along the snow fence around the site, the residents went back to their shanties about 3:30 A.M. to get what sleep they could.

Sunday began with a hot breakfast, the first in the City's history, which the staff had made arrangements for in the space of a few hours. Following a cleanup campaign through the City, Rev. Abernathy led a long service at the culture tent in his own black Southern Baptist style. His sermon, entitled "The Way Out of a Dilemma," was based on the biblical story of three lepers, left by their countrymen to die outside the gates of their city. The lepers debated what they should do, concluding it was impossible to return to their city, and pointless to sit rotting where they were. They decided at length that their only hope was to press forward into the wilderness where they knew enemy armies were camped, in the hope that God might make friends for them with the soldiers. God did even better than that, however, by putting panic in the enemy general's mind so that he and his troops fled precipitately, leaving behind all their food and valuables, which the lepers then enjoyed.

Abernathy saw the story as symbolic of the plight of poor people. He had preached this sermon at least once before in Washington that summer, at the historic New York Avenue Presbyterian Church near the White House, whose pastor, Dr. George Docherty, was an old friend of the movement. Dr. Docherty's congregation was predominantly white, and his sanctuary well-appointed and dignified. In this setting Rev. Abernathy's delivery had been relatively restrained, containing little of the music characteristic of the black Baptist style. But in the tent this Sunday, surrounded by several score brotherly faces of mostly older, deep-South campaigners who had stayed in the City through all its trials, Abernathy let out the stops. "I came to the District of Columbia," he said, "to go to jail and I will go on the morrow. I been to jail 19 times. But everytime I go there, God was there ahead of me. . . .

"There is a dilemma in the world and in the nation. And," he confessed, "there is a dilemma in Resurrection City. Honesty impels me to say we're not all doing the right thing. There are some here who are weights around our neck. . . . Some of our strongest supporters are white, yet several of them came to me to tell me they were beaten and robbed."

Though he was tired and did not come across with anything like the spirit and grace Rev. C. L. Franklin had displayed two nights earlier, he still knew how to move his people, and he did. One elderly campaigner, a small gray-haired woman from Montgomery, Alabama, who had known Abernathy as far back as the bus boycott in 1956 was moved into what is called a shout. Leaping from her seat, she waved her arms and screamed frenzied hosannas until other worshippers grabbed her and held her in a seat, where she struggled and continued frequent cries until worn out. No one was surprised at her action; in fact, one got the feeling it was regarded as a good sign, indicating that Abernathy had not lost touch with these, his people, and that the Holy Spirit was still moving among them in their present time of trials.

By now, the Interior Department had made it official that the permit would not be extended. But there was no word about when the government would move to evict the campers, only hints that the permit provision for a "reasonable time" for dismantling the camp would be respected. After the conclusion of the service, Abernathy and most of the top staff went into more strategy sessions, while other staff kept watch at the camp's main gates to forestall any confrontations with the corps of watching police. As the permit's 8:00 P.M. deadline came and went, TV newsmen posed solemnly in front of their cameras to report that the area was calm; visitors and residents gathered in groups around the gate eyeing the police warily. There were no serious incidents. Hosea Williams mounted the hood of a car and harangued the crowd briefly, asking them to go home and rejoin the marchers in the morning: "Tomorrow will be a strange day in history," he shouted. "Tomorrow all of us are going to jail; tomorrow some will be beaten; tomorrow some will be killed." He condemned troublemakers in the camp as "paid, lowdown and dirty," and said, "If anyone wants to throw rocks at the police, go do it, but for God's sake go over on the other side of the fence."

The City had endured a full complement of robberies, assaults and one shooting during the day, but perhaps because everyone had been up almost all of Saturday night, Sunday evening was quiet, almost placid. Before dawn Monday morning, rain returned to the camp one final time.

6

Doomsday

The workshop promised for 3:00 P.M. Sunday by Bevel and Jackson did not come off; inquirers were told it had been re-scheduled for 6:00 P.M., and then for 9:00 P.M., but the two staff never showed up, possibly because there was no set-tled strategy to report that evening. The leadership did not expect the Administration to take action against their shanty-town at least until later in the week. Thus they were caught by surprise when word came, well after midnight, that a mas-sive police force would be on hand early Monday morning to turn them out. They were uncertain about how to meet the confrontation, and some reports say the debate was long and bitter. Abernathy had vowed again and again that he would not abandon the campsite voluntarily, and such a stance ob-viously called for a stand in the City. But, as staff members later admitted, the violence in the camp had made it all too clear that, in Andrew Young's phrase, "We just couldn't be sure of our troops." There were rumors of arsenals hidden in the maze of shanties and of plans by "jitterbugs" to attack police as they moved through the City.

This lack of control made a stand in the camp extremely risky. Yet it would be humiliating if they simply abandoned the site in the face of a police show of force. At length a compromise was worked out, and by sunrise the staff was ready.

Monday, June 24, looked like Doomsday. A heavy, dark-gray overcast hung low over the City. The air was hot, thick and hazy, muffling noise of the rush-hour traffic that had been diverted away from the Park. Rain seemed imminent all morning but never came. The Reflecting Pool was still and glossy, the beech trees alongside it unmoving except for a few stray branches, like statues with nervous tics. Lincoln's columns stood pale and spectral against the sky. The plywood of the shanties was wet and shining, mud was once more inches deep. The residents came awake sluggishly, subdued by the atmosphere and their own apprehensions.

Abernathy read a statement to the press about 8:30 A.M.: "We state now as we have stated before: we will not leave our homes in this city voluntarily. We will honor the permit granted us by the Indians, who hold a more rightful claim to the land than the government of the United States.... We therefore plan to remain here and continue with our Poor People's Campaign to demand from the departments of government and the Congress food for hungry people, jobs for the jobless, decent, safe and sanitary housing for every family and a floor under the income of all Americans.

"Immediately following this press briefing I will pay a visit to the Department of Agriculture and Secretary Freeman.... I will tell him there is more that he can do, and that he must do it now. From there I will go to the Congress, to ask to be heard by both the House and the Senate on this hunger question.... I must remind them that one-fifth of this nation goes to bed hungry every night while we pay farmers not to grow food, while we store food in barns and even dump it in the ocean.... It is likely that I will be arrested and my people with me, but the problem of hunger is so great, therefore our cause is so just that we will gladly accept whatever penalty is imposed upon us for doing the work we must do.

"No matter what happens to me or to Resurrection City, the Poor People's Campaign will go on.... We are in Washington to stay until the people of America speak and until the Congress acts on this critical issue.

"I leave here now to be about this important work. I invite all who believe with me to join me on this journey to the Department of Agriculture, to the Capitol and even to jail if this is where the road leads."

By 9:20 the lines had formed and he led at least 200 marchers through the city from west to east, past the fence and across 17th Street, towards Washingon's spike and the buildings beyond. The people were told to leave their belongings packed in their shanties, because the government had agreed to identify and store them so they could get them back when released from jail.

Crossing the street, the campaigners saw a line of city busses begin discharging long columns of police. In minutes, several hundred men in gray uniforms were crowded along the sidewalk. Abernathy commented that the scene "looks like Russia...I never saw anything like that in Mississippi." Then urging the marchers to "look at me, not at them," he led them on to the Agriculture Department, where Jesse Jackson exhorted the crowd while he tried unsuccessfully to meet with Secretary Freeman. From there he proceeded to Constitution Avenue and 1st Street, S.E., at the edge of the Capitol grounds, where a solid phalanx of police blocked the way.

Capitol Police Chief John Powell would not let the group on the Capitol grounds. He spoke like a textbook on good police-community relations: "For those of you who have made a decision to be arrested, we will be as patient and systematic in handling you if arrested as we can."

Abernathy was insistent: "Will you please let us through? People are dying of starvation."

Powell was unmoved.

"This is our Capitol," Abernathy said. "We pay taxes, we maintain it, we keep it up. These are our Senators and our Congressmen. What have you got against this group? Why are you discriminating? Because we are poor? All we ask is the right to go on this ground. I beg you not to deny us that right...just far enough to get the whole group on the steps." The discussion went on for nearly an hour, but he was still not allowed to pass. Finally Abernathy told his group to sit down.

At noon Chief Powell took up his bullhorn: "It has become necessary that we make arrests. We do not want to....I ask that you remain calm." His men set up a table in the street and an arrest team began processing the "arrestees." Abernathy was among the first, flashing a V for Victory sign as he was led away to a waiting jail bus. The other marchers cheered wildly; they were happy at last to have the chance to go to jail. With the arrest team operating briskly and efficiently some 230 arrests were completed by 2:00 P.M. and the streetcorner was cleared.

At Resurrection City, well over 1,500 policemen (officials avoided giving a definite figure) had the site entirely surrounded by 9:45 A.M. The staff had wanted only 18 residents to stay, but about 110 residents remained in the camp, sloshing through the mud, some carrying battered cardboard boxes tied with string and full of secondhand clothes. Most of them gathered in the culture tent, where Hosea Williams led them in freedom songs and exhorted them to stay nonviolent when the police came. Trusted marshals circulated through the shantytown to coax stragglers from their shacks and keep an eye out for suspicious people or "infiltrators." About 9:45 a police sound car began driving up and down the length of the camp along Independence Avenue, which was closed to other traffic, with a black policeman speaking into the microphone: "The permit on this property has expired. You must leave here within the next 56 minutes to avoid arrest and prosecution. For those of you who have no other means of transportation, bus service to your homes will be provided at no cost by the Travelers Aid Society. Shuttle busses are now available at the west side of the Reflecting Pool." A trickle of people accepted the offer, walking slowly past the police lines with their cargo of suitcases and boxes and sitting in a group on the west side of the Lincoln Memorial. Soon after the sound car began, the police closed their line and ordered most newsmen to get behind it. Williams began leading freedom songs over the PA system. While the minutes wore on, the sound car's pronouncements were mixed with echoing verses of "Oh Johnson, You Never Can Jail Us All," "Aint Gona Let Nobody Turn Me Round," and "This Could Be the Last Time."

At 11:10 a workman mounted the main power pole and clipped the wires, cutting off the PA system in mid-chorus. A few minutes later a line of police, members of the District's elite Civil Disturbance Unit, moved into the City from the east. The police wore riot helmets, flak jackets, and knee-high rubber boots, and were armed with shotguns, two types of tear gas grenades, pistols, and billy clubs. They banged on the shanties with gun butts, calling for anyone inside to come out, then searched the empty shacks. They found no people and no weapons, though one or two shacks with boards nailed over their exits were boobytrapped and caught fire when the officers forced them open, and in another a tear gas grenade went off. The campaigners waiting at the camp's center went to the jail busses singing peacefully. One wonders how the police felt approaching their target as if it were Ho Chi Minh's headquarters; they looked a little overdressed. Within an hour the campsite was cleared and sealed off.

Hosea Williams posted bond at the D.C. General Sessions Court a few hours after his arrest. "We got things to do," he told newsmen. He watched a jail bus swing around a corner. "That bus just took Abernathy and 170 other people to jail. But we will prevail. We certainly are in a new phase now."

What did he think of the city's closing? "We got trapped down in that mudhole. I want to thank the government for getting us out of it. My talent is in the movement. Now that Resurrection City is gone, we can focus on the real problems — with Congress, for instance — instead of wasting half our energy trying to keep kids from throwing rocks."

Williams had been opposed to the shantytown idea from the beginning. But Andrew Young, who was to serve as chief spokesman for SCLC while Abernathy was in jail, echoed his sentiments at an afternoon press conference: "In one sense," he said, "whoever ran us out maybe did us a great favor." But, he pointed out, "We never said this was supposed to be a city of saints. We said: Here are the poor, America. See for yourself." He predicted arrests would continue through the rest of the week, "and possibly the next week and the next." The following day 300 people from Philadelphia would arrive in the capital, he added, to demonstrate and join the others in jail. Young also asserted that SCLC would now turn to massive nationwide boycotts to pressure business leaders into support for their demands. "We are going to try to withdraw as much support from the economy as possible."

Jesse Jackson, who as head of Operation Breadbasket had conducted many successful consumer boycotts under SCLC's auspices, was in charge of the boycott planning. He spoke of the rationale of boycotting in detail while paying tribute to Resurrection City at Monday night's mass meeting:

"Tonight our City is under seige. Our City has been taken over by more than 3,000 military policemen from Pharoah's

army. ["Uh, huh," "that's right."] Now I do not get angry
with Pharoah — because with his blinded perceptions he has
tried to occupy a City that he knows nothing about except
its location.... [But] Resurrection City at its very best is not
a mudhole on the *mall* ["Well"], but Resurrection City is
God's hand in history.... I looked in retrospect, after we had
moved this morning: the camp had been taken over and as
I went down Pennsylvania Avenue I saw the proximity
of Resurrection City — the home of lovers and of tired people
who are coming with a decent proposition — and I found that
we were just about a thousand yards from the White House.
And I was a bit sad because they had taken it over. And
then I said that, 'But you *know,* for seven weeks, the Lord
has prepared a table before us in the *presence* of our enemies!' [Applause.]

"The real problem that the military had is that it has attempted to take its *fist* and smack the wind; it has attempted
to take its body and stand against the onslaught of rushing
waters; it has attempted to make time go backwards — it has
attempted to take a baby when the water has broken
["Talk!"], send it back into its mother's womb; they have
tried to take a bulldozer and tried to turn around an *idea.*
. . . [Applause.]

"I want you to hear this well, 'cause this is what we're
gonna do: We're gonna set up Poor People's Campaign committees in 40 of the nation's cities. Hear me well: In each
of these cities we are going to boycott [scattered applause],
we're going to boycott the downtown areas. What does that
mean? The reason we have been ignored is because no one
has been hurting but the poor people [applause], therefore
we've got to go into a theory I call Redistribution of the Pain.
["Yessir!"] In other words, when *downtown* Memphis is
boycotted ["Umhum"]; when the Loop in Chicago is boycotted ["Yeah!"]; when downtown Los *Angeles* is boycotted;
then the *Chamber of Commerce* of those cities will find the

best interest of the poor people to the self-interest of their
city. In other words, because you were sinkin' you reached
up and grabbed the city by its *v*itals ["Yeah!"] and pulled
it down with ya. Everybody's hurtin' then. ["Yeah!" Applause.] Y'all understand what I'm sayin'? ["Yeah!!"] Y'all see
which way we goin'?" ["Yeah!"]

These remarks and subsequent events make it plain that,
relieved of the millstone in West Potomac Park, the Campaign leadership expected to get on with its strategy of mass
arrests and boycotts. The multi-ethnic coalition was now
definitely a thing of the past. No Mexican-Americans joined
Abernathy's pilgrimage to jail, and none of their leaders
were seen participating in Campaign activities thereafter.
Rudolfo "Corky" Gonzalez had, in fact, returned to Denver
in disgust and discouragement before the camp was closed,
and only a few of Reies Tijerina's followers remained with
him at Hawthorne School. SCLC's actions were now directed
exclusively at black people and white liberals, members of
the old civil rights movement's constituency.

Mass arrests were essential to the strategy, as the leadership
made clear in several statements."Those of us who demonstrate...must become organizers and evangelists," James
Bevel told a mass meeting on June 25. "Now we've split up
teams for the four sections (of Washington)....I want you
to hear me good now. The *teams* gonna set up [in] *churches,*
start organizing *people,* and each team gonna organize about
a thousand or 2,000 folks for jail from *Wash*ington.

"Now somebody said, 'What's the purpose of that?' The
purpose is *this*: If you asked Negroes to boycott tonight, they
wouldn't do it, would they? ["No!"] But if you put about a
thousand of their children and mothers and cousins in *jail,*
they will boycott downtown 'til the *meat* rots on the shelves!"
[Applause, shouts of "Soul Power!"] Jesse Jackson, asked to
estimate the boycotts' chances of having the desired political
effect, echoed the same feeling: "It will probably be in pro-

portion to the amount of people that go to jail. Jail has an amazing way of sensitizing a nation to the fact that something urgent is happening."

Bevel, still in charge of mobilizing Washington, repeated this contention as he stumped the District's black sections over the next two weeks. Rev. Abernathy issued a letter from his jail cell the day following his arrest, addressed to "the clergymen of America." It called on them to converge on the Capitol in large numbers for "another confrontation with the government" in which they would be "the first waves of people who are willing to join the poor in jail. Other waves will follow, but we need the inspirational example of as many clergymen as possible. Words are no longer sufficient." For the rest of the week Andrew Young continued to predict to newsmen that hundreds of sympathizers were coming to the District to join his leader in jail.

In this effort SCLC was attempting to create a situation similar to that which developed in Selma. After the 600 unarmed marchers were attacked by police on the Edmund Pettus Bridge, Dr. King issued a similar call for help, and the response was both overwhelming and surprising. Within 24 hours after the call was sent out, several thousand ministers, priests, nuns and bishops were pouring into Selma's astonished black community to join it for the dramatic second march to the bridge two days later. In Washington, it was evident by the end of the week that nothing of this sort was about to happen again. Young predicted 300 marchers from Philadelphia would be marching on the Capitol grounds on Tuesday, the day after the camp was closed; on Tuesday no one showed up, but SCLC made do by parading its mule train through the downtown section of the city and predicting the Philadelphians would arrive Wednesday. On Wednesday 35 persons followed Jesse Jackson onto the Capitol grounds, but scrupulously obeyed police instructions to break up into three groups, thus avoiding arrests. Thursday about 60 persons from Washington gathered at the Campaign's "Action Center" for a march; but it was called off, perhaps because of the small turnout and perhaps because Rev. Abernathy was holding a press conference at the D.C. jail that afternoon.

The next arrest demonstration came on Friday, June 28. Four hundred quiet, neatly dressed Quakers drove to Washington from their General Conference in Cape May, New Jersey, to demonstrate support for the Campaign. Most of the group formed a silent, legal vigil line on the west side of 1st Street across from the Capitol grounds. Then about 35 of their number, all of them white, crossed the street and walked up the wide steps, sitting down in a plaza beneath a statue of John Marshall to hold a silent Meeting for worship. This was in clear violation of Capitol regulations, and Capitol police closed in on them; but after taking a sign reading "Quaker Meeting for Worship" from one of their young men, the police withdrew and did not interfere as, in the manner of Quaker meetings, one member and then another rose to sing, pray and quote Scripture as each felt led to do so.

After the Quakers had been sitting for some time, another group of about 40 demonstrators, mostly black, mounted the steps past them, singing and clapping. The police let them walk all the way to the top of the steps, where they tried to enter some blocked doors. Then they turned and started back down the long flights of steps to the street; but the police surrounded them when they reached the John Marshall plaza and began arresting them, still ignoring the silent circle nearby.

The Quakers knew they were violating Capitol regulations, and were expecting to be arrested also. They did not at first understand what was happening. But after several of the blacks had been processed by the ubiquitous "arrest team" and placed in a jail bus with still no move being made against

them, their leader, Ross Flanagan of New York, realized that
the police intended to let his all-white group "demonstrate"
undisturbed. The obvious double standard in the police action was too much for him. When the Meeting for Worship
was concluded with the customary exchange of handshakes,
Flanagan told the Friends that he could not stand idly by
and let the police action go unchallenged. He walked over,
pushed past the police line into the SCLC group and was
followed a moment later by the rest of the Quakers. They
were met with cheers from the other group and were arrested in their turn.

The arrest total for Friday was 78 persons. It was the largest single number of arrests after the closing of Resurrection
City. The 35 Quakers were the only group from outside
Washington which actually came to court arrest. On only
two other occasions after Resurrection City's closing did the
Campaign provoke arrests: on the 4th of July, 24 were arrested near the Capitol trying to stage a watermelon "eat-in";
on the 9th of July, 18 were arrested, again on the Capitol
grounds. Eight other demonstrations connected with the
Campaign were conducted after the last week of June. The
largest of these were marches around — not on — the Capitol
grounds by a largely white group of ministers, priests and
nuns from the Capitol region on four succeeding Sundays
from June 30 to July 21. These marchers were extremely
careful to avoid arrests; they carried no signs and broke into
such small groups as they approached the Capitol that their
ranks were largely indistinguishable from the crowds of
weekend tourists. None of the other four demonstrations
drew more than 60 participants, and one of these was nearly
all children.

As these figures suggest, Black Washington's response to
the call to fill the jails was sparse. The organizing teams
spread out into the neighborhoods, the mass meetings con-

tinued, but only rarely were the churches full, and very few stepped forward to confront the government. SCLC leaders charged that Administration pressure was being applied to keep Washingtonians away from the Campaign. Little evidence of pressure was ever presented, and what pressure there may have been was probably minor, because it was largely unnecessary. The Campaign had no momentum; it had failed both as a moral crusade and as entertainment. Solidarity Day and the arrests of Rev. Abernathy were not sufficient to offset the movement's dullness and uncertain virtue. Black Washington was, according to all available evidence, simply indifferent to the movement; to them it was already over.

As early as June 30 Andrew Young was very close to admitting this to certain people, and was revising the official version of the Campaign's objectives. He told the *New York Times* in an exclusive interview on that date, "It really looks as though we'll have difficulty pulling through with anything. The way it reads now, we got our rumps kicked in Washington." He agreed that his staff was "probably in over our head," in Washington. But he was not discouraged. "It's like you're fighting preliminaries all of your life.... Even Russia doesn't have the confidence and power to take on the United States government, and that is exactly what we're trying to do. Win, lose or draw," he went on, "the fact that you are in the championships means that you are better off than when you were in the preliminaries. I think that success is to show that we wage a good fight. We don't have to win this one. We just have to show that we can do battle."

Rev. Young was not as candid when he spoke later that same day to the first of the four Sunday marches of the clergy. "The Poor People's Campaign," he told them, "is running just about like any other campaign we've ever run. That is, it runs along for a month or six weeks, and then we're in real deep trouble. America will tolerate protest — for

a week or two. And if you'll remember reading the newspapers, all the editorials in the beginning were favorable and
then they began to take a little twist and they began to find
fault with everything but poverty. And right now they have
decided that we have made our point and we should go home
and let them get back to business as usual.

"Well — that's when the fight starts. And so I want to say
that one of the things we are saying here today is that the
Poor People's Campaign is not over, it's just moving into the
second phase. [Applause.] Phase one was basically a poor
people's phase: we went to great effort to see to it that the
students didn't come in and overrun the poor people, that all
of our good middle-class white friends didn't come in and
take over the Campaign from the poor people, that even
SCLC as a staff didn't dominate the Campaign, but that
somehow in the first phase of the Campaign, the poor people
themselves would have an opportunity to demonstrate the
issues by their very presence and speak to them in any way
they saw fit.

"Now what you saw at Resurrection City was the message
that poor people had to give to the country. It was not a
message of the religious poor; it was not a message of the
emotionally stable poor; it was not a message of the sweet
and decent poor; it was a message of the poor. Poor folks —
anyway they came — we took 'em in. [Applause.]

"Now, I think that we have to go into Phase Two where we
admit as middle-class people that *poverty* is not a problem of
the poor; that poverty is a problem of the nation.... [Poor
people] are now standing at the door of the Promised Land.
And somehow that Promised Land is symbolized by that
Capitol we're going to march around. And just as Joshua
marched around the walls of Jericho seven times, I think
we ought to march around that Capitol seven times too.
[Applause.] But I don't think we ought to march all seven
times today. [Laughter and applause.]...Maybe [today's

march] might set something in motion so that by the third
or fourth week when we march around the additional times,
we might see some of the walls of opposition, some of the
walls which lock the poor out of our own society begin to
come tumblin' down.

"Now that's all we're gonna do; and it doesn't *seem* like
it's very militant.... [But] I'm more concerned with power
than I am with militance; and I have learned in some eight
or ten years in this movement that there's nothin' more
*pow*erful than a silent spiritual army.... You don't have to
talk *bad* about [Senator James] Eastland: you have to *walk*
around his house and *pray* for him." [Extended applause.]
He encouraged them to go to jail with the Campaign and to
support the "economic withdrawals" the Campaign would
soon initiate.

The highly-educated white liberal audience seemed anxious
to believe Rev. Young's remarks. Yet almost none of his statements were accurate: the Poor People's Campaign was not
running "just about like" SCLC's other campaigns. Most
early editorials were not favorable to the movement. The
SCLC staff did indeed dominate the Campaign's early phase.
College students were expected to join the movement early,
by the thousands, and middle-class whites were not kept out
of the Campaign at any point except by inefficiency and en-
demic hostility. What he described as Phase One was anything except what the leadership had planned and hoped it
would be. SCLC also demonstrably considered boycotts and
mass arrests — among other things — considerably more potent
than the prayerful plodding of any "silent spiritual army."
Yet there were no signs among the 600 professional men and
women in the audience (or among any of the reporters present, for that matter) that any of them penetrated or even perceived this patent humbug.

In view of these comments, it should be noted that Rev.
Young's *Times* interview was no fluke. The same rhetoric

showed up frequently in his statements after June 30. On
Tuesday, July 2, he spoke to a boycott planning meeting of
black preachers from several cities at St. Stephen's Baptist
Church in Washington, telling them, "We are in a low
period now. We have done basically what we came here to
do. The truth of it is we have done all that we know how
to do, and we're standin' here waitin' on the mercy and the
power of God to deliver us.... We know that this whole
nation is on the verge of destruction; and we know that we
are perhaps the *only* people that might redeem it.... We
were fightin' preliminary battles in Birmingham: Bull Connor was a chump; Jim Clark was a rookie; we went through
them in nothin' flat. But we dared, under the inspiration of
Dr. Martin Luther King and now under the leadership of
Ralph Abernathy to do somethin' that *Russia* doesn't have
nerve to do: we *jumped* the United States government. And
that's the big league. We are fighting for the heavyweight
championship of the *world,* and we are fighting to see which
is more powerful: military power or soul power. ["Go 'head!"]
Now I know that soul power is more powerful ["Go 'head!"];
but it may be that we don't know enough about it yet, so military power *might* knock us out now. But we *will* have fought
a good fight.... So that's where we are, and I don't care
about a victory. I don't care whether we win or lose. I don't
see SCLC on trial. I don't see nonviolence on trial — I don't
see truth on trial."

Such talk could hardly have been designed to fire up the
ministers who came there to help begin the Campaign's most
serious effort. This meeting was the major black response to
Rev. Abernathy's call for a clergymen's confrontation nationwide; the group was small, did not represent many cities, and
made no attempt to demonstrate. In the discussion that followed Rev. Young's remarks, the visiting preachers rose one
after another to detail the problems facing boycott efforts in
their home cities: in one place the SCLC representatives

were not respected by the community; in another, there were
a number of groups competing for the leadership; a third
explained his city's difficulties in obtaining consistent information or cooperation from the Campaign's Washington headquarters; and several nodded agreement with a fourth who
explained that his community was not even aware of the
boycott plans.

By July 7, at the second of the clergy's Sunday marches,
Rev. Young admitted privately that the Campaign's impact
on public opinion had been so minimal that the boycotts had
no real chance of mobilizing the support necessary for them
to get off the ground.

It is quite possible that the SCLC leadership had by July
7 already decided to end the Washington Campaign, judging
by what the Rev. Young told the Resurrection City refugees
staying at Hawthorne School that evening.

Approximately 150 men, women and children were staying
at Hawthorne, people who had not gone to jail or who had
served only short sentences. They were there primarily because SCLC had been unable to find any other quarters for
them; it is not clear whether the inability was due to the
staff's demonstrated inefficiency or because the stream of volunteers from Washington had simply dried up; probably
both. The families there sat and grumbled through their
days in crowded, less than sanitary conditions. On June 26
the District Department of Licenses and Permits had threatened to have the refugees evicted, but relented after a conference with the school's owners, probably because there was no
place else for the people to go.

The violence that undermined Resurrection City followed
these people to the school, and now there was even less
diversion for the "jitterbugs" as the Campaign faltered
through these weeks. At night the place often became bed-
lam, with drunks fighting each other and threatening the

families, thefts and attempted rapes frequent and noise constant. SCLC was probably moved to act only when the school's owners informed them that they were leaving the country on July 10 and that the building had to be cleared and closed by the 9th. Rev. Young arrived about 11:00 P.M. Sunday night to tell the people what was to happen to them next.

It took some effort to get the people quiet enough for him to speak. When they were settled in the auditorium on steel and fiberglass school-chairs, he began by telling them of the short time they had had to get out of the camp. This created problems, he said, "because Northern people don't open up their houses the way Southern folks do. We never had to live in a hotel in any of our work in the South [which was not true]. But Northern people just aren't hospitable [which was not true either]."

Because of this, he went on, SCLC was not going to be able to find housing for all those remaining in Washington. And since Congress was going home in about two weeks anyway, the leadership was now considering ways of influencing Congressmen in their home districts. One idea they were kicking around was that of having a project in Wilbur Mills' home district; another idea was to send black families to white districts in Iowa, Montana, and other Northern states to help elect favorable condidates or defeat unfavorable ones. And so on. (He did not mention the boycotts.) But during the next week all of them, he said, would be asked to do one of three things: first, go home and organize there; second, stay in D.C. with a smaller group to continue mobilizing its black community; and third, if they had no home to go back to, to settle somewhere besides Washington, with SCLC assistance.

None of this, he insisted, meant that the Poor People's Campaign was over, pointing out that it took four years of struggle to integrate Southern lunch counters, and poverty was a much tougher fight. "We will probably be in Washington for the next year or so in one form or another."

He agreed the Campaign had problems, but felt these were outweighed even by the immediate gains it had produced. "Whatever it's cost us, it's worth it." He referred to the Bonus Marchers of the Depression who were run out of the Capitol seemingly without achieving anything; yet within a few years, the New Deal had enacted most of their demands. He spoke of how there had to be some time between seed time and harvest, noting that it wasn't until a year after the Birmingham campaign and six months after the Selma march that Congress had passed the legislation the campaigners had called for. He predicted that by December, 1968, the Department of Agriculture would be issuing free food stamps to people who couldn't afford to buy them, and said:

"You know, rich white folks are funny. They know we're right, but if they give us some of the things we're asking for now, they'd be admitting we were right and they were wrong. But if we let things quiet down a little, they'll start doing some of these things and say they were meaning to do them all along."

SCLC hoped, he continued, to establish a permanent Poor People's Embassy in Washington. This statement drew the evening's only applause. But they couldn't do that, he added, while trying to run an operation like the one here at Hawthorne. He compared the Campaign to a boxing match: "We been through Round One, and now we've got to go back to our corner to rest up and get ready for Round Two." Then he opened the floor for questions.

Some of them were vaguely suspicious. One young black man asked him if what he had said meant for them to go home.

Rev. Young said yes, it did.

Well how, the young man asked, were they supposed to go home when all their clothes and belongings had been left in

Resurrection City and confiscated by the government. (The Administration did not mark the boxes as it promised to do, and between it and SCLC's primitive storage facilities most residents lost everything they left behind.)

Rev. Young said, "I don't know."

Well, why doesn't somebody pay us for our clothes?

Who?

Whoever told us we'd get them back.

In Gandhi's campaigns, Rev. Young replied, he made everyone sign a slip saying they were responsible not only for themselves and their belongings but also for their own way back.

The youth's response was trenchant: "Gandhi," he said simply, "wasn't on *this* march."

Rev. Young said that it was easy enough to see the Campaign's mistakes now, in retrospect; but in the beginning, no one had ever run a Poor People's Campaign before and so they had just to do their best and make their mistakes.

Two nights later Hawthorne was empty. Some residents crowded into a private home for a few days; some went to a seminary in Alexandria, Virginia; most went home. The dozen or so in Alexandria were evicted by the Seminary two days later and spent at least one night on the lawn in front of its gates. They then walked 12 miles into the District, demanding housing from SCLC. The Campaign's liaison man from the National Council of Churches rented rooms for them in an expensive hotel. Ultimately this group built a small tent city of its own in Northern Virginia, and after living there for several weeks left for Selma, Alabama, to begin construction of its own community on land donated to them by Mrs. Amelia Platts Boynton, a distinguished Alabama civil rights leader.

James Bevel and Jesse Jackson continued mass meetings and boycott planing well into the second week of July. But then they dropped out of public view, and second echelon

staff like Albert Sampson conducted the meetings. Attend-
ance was declining steadily, demonstrations were few and
of little moment. As the 350 jailed with Abernathy were
released over the span of two weeks, they quickly got the
message Rev. Young had given those at Hawthorne, and
straggled home. The SCLC office at the Trailways bus depot
which was issuing bus tickets turned out to be as efficient an
operation as the Campaign had produced. By the 10th, when
Hawthorne School was locked up, it was evident that SCLC
operations in the city were being phased out. Many lower
echelon staff did not yet know where they were headed from
here; but all were making plans and some were already gone.

Abernathy's 20-day sentence was up on July 13. The remaining staff wanted to make an event of his release and the
final mass meeting was devoted to mobilizing support for it.
The meeting was held at the First Baptist Church of Deanwood, a middle-class black neighborhood in northeast Washington. A mobilizing team spent three days canvassing prior
to the meeting, urging the people to attend, yet only fifty
people from the community showed up and they were a
tepid, undemonstrative group. The freedom singing was half-
hearted, the responsive "Wells" and "Amens" to the speakers
muted, people were leaving in ones and twos through the
last hour and a half. Neither Jackson nor Bevel was on hand.
Mr. Jimmy Wilson, an SCLC field worker from Chicago,
spoke first, looking proud but somewhat incongruous in the
pulpit with his bushy natural haircut, African robe and beads.
He was followed by Hosea Williams. Hosea was feeling
expansive that night and he preached long, hard, and, in
his way, brilliantly. "I can honestly say," he began, "that
I've been in the civil rights movement a long time. I consider
myself a veteran. I've been through many battles and I've
faced death many times. But I can honestly say that the Poor
People's Campaign is probably the most significant thing

that man has done or that man has attempted to do since
Moses led the children out of Egypt land. I have often said
that Martin Luther King is the greatest man that has lived
since the birth of Jesus Christ." [Applause.]

A few moments later Hosea was worked up; the words
were pouring from his mouth and his face was running with
perspiration. In the heat of oratory, he revised his estimate
of the movement's significance: "The Poor People's Campaign is about the greatest thing that God has ever charged
unto mankind. Now I know this but some of you don't know
this. I don't know anything that God has ever asked man to
do was any more *important* than the Poor People's Campaign.
Let me tell you about the Poor People's Campaign. This is
the greatest thing that God has asked man to *do* in the *history* of the world. I don't know *any*thing that God has asked
man to do any greater than the Poor People's Campaign. It's
much greater than what God charged Moses to do, to go on
back down into Egypt land...."

Each time Hosea began a paragraph with "Let me tell you
about the Poor People's Campaign," he soon veered off after
a few sentences into a long aside about slavery, segregation, or
some allied topic. An example: "I sat in jail one time 60 long
days, and I started talkin' to God. I asked God these questions: God, if you're such a *just* God; God, if you're such
a *good* God; God, if you are such a *righteous* God—I have
committed no crime. Why should I have to labor here in
the hole of the Chatham County Jail, eatin' light bread and
drinkin' water? Why should I have my *only* friends as rats
and roaches? What *crime*, God, have I committed? I've *only*
done Thy will and you've let them incarcerate me, take me
away from my wife and my children, while the Ku Klux
Klan walks the streets in harmony. I said, *You* supposed to be
such a *righteous* God, *tell me*, what have I done? *You* don't
bother the Ku Klux Klan, *God*, they walkin' the streets
free; *I'm* the only one here in a prison cell.

"Then an angel spoke to me. He said, 'Hosea' — and I'm not lyin' baby, they spoke to me; if they'd spoke to *you,* you'd a'been down there in Resurrection City! [Laughter and applause.] Then they reminded me, they said, 'Hosea, you aren't suff'rin'.... You not suff'rin', Hosea,' they said. *'Think* of some of those black folks that was captured against their own will and *crammed* down in the *holds* o' ships! Think of the mothers that gave birth to *babies* that *died* while their heads was in their husbands arms!' — He said, 'Hosea, you ain't suff'rin'! Hosea, you oughta think of the slaves ... think of the women who labored *nine* months with a baby, then to give birth prayin' to the Lord, *"Please* don't let my baby be born," for fear she didn't know what moment the white man would come to the *hut* and *snatch* the baby away from her, and sell it on the slave block — like it was a *chicken,* or like it was a *pig!'* Then I thought about the black men, how it was dangerous to love their own black women 'cause they didn't know what time the white man would come to the hut and *snatch* the *shutter* away, take his black woman away, take her out and sell her like she was a cow or like she was a duck. 'Hosea, you ain't suffered yet.' Then I started thinkin', through *suffering* there's *growth.* That's why we're so big, baby, we've suffered. Through *suffering* there's *wisdom!* Through *suffering* there's power. No longer can white folks make us *bow* down. We shall say to them from now until eternity, 'It is all over!'

"And this," Hosea continued, "is what I wanta tell you about the Poor People's Campaign. We had them scared unto death. We had Johnson not knowing which way he could go. We had Rockefeller and we had Kennedy and we had *Ford,* we had the *Du* Ponts thinking, 'It's all over.'"

Then he was off on another tangent, this time about the troubles his mother had had in Georgia.

"Folks," he went on a few moments later, "just let me tell you about the Poor People's Campaign. After they killed Dr.

King, they had to admit this, and I have to admit this — Dr. King had the greatest staff that man has ever been able to assemble. SCLC had a greater staff even than Jesus *Christ* had: ain't *no*body on our staff would've sold Dr. King for 30 pieces of silver. *Nobody.* But I'm not worried. They've got us reelin' and they got us rockin'! Truth crushed to earth will rise again. I'm still not worried."

Several more digressions later, he began making specific claims: the police planted crates of tear gas by the campsite to provoke further incidents. A volunteer engineer helping with construction — "he must have been sent by the CIA," Hosea insisted — left two cases of molotov cocktails in a shanty he built. "I'll tell you something else I found out too: all them white folks you read about gettin' beat in Resurrection City? Almost every white man got *beat,* the Negro that beat him got $5.00. Almost every white man got *robbed,* the black boy that *robbed* him got $5.00. I'm tellin' you how *low* the government will stoop, I never be*lieved* my country would stop so low. . . . The newspapers just *lied.* I never *seen* papers like the Washington *Post* and the Washington *Star* stoop to such a low ebb!" He asserted that reporters had been planted to ask Rev. Abernarthy irrelevant questions, and that governmental pressure was being put on local preachers to keep them from cooperation with the movement.

Then another detour: "Resurrection City has been a great thing. God knows I've learned *so* much. I saw a black man one day, for instance, just knock a white man *down,* just bust the man in the *face,* hard as he could with his fist. And I walked up to this black man, I couldn't understand his bein' so savage and so beastly. I said, 'Why did you do that? *All* white people are *not* our enemies, *some* white people are our friends. Much of the money we spend here, white people gave to us; many of the beatings we take here, white people take 'em. Why would you do this?' And let me tell you somethin'; in a long conversation this black man told me this, he said,

'Mr. Williams, now I'm from Mississippi, and you don't understand. *Every* since I was a little boy,' he said, 'about three times in my life I saw white men beat my father when my father really hadn't done nothin'.' He said, 'One time I saw a white man *kick* and *slap* my own mother.' He said, 'Twice in my life I've been beat by white men and was scared to fight back. And I said to myself if I *ever* get out of Mississippi, I was gonna beat me a white man.' [Laughter and applause.]

"Now, friends, let me tell you about the Poor People's Campaign." But first another aside: "I'm gonna tell you something. I don't bow to *man,* I bow to what *God* created. One of Dr. King's last sermons, I remember he preached, it was in Marks, Mississippi. And these black women came runnin' and cryin' to Dr. King and showin' him their babies, they looked like skeletons, and cryin' and pleadin' to Dr. King, 'Please help us, Dr. King.' Some said, 'I haven't had a job in three years.' Some said, 'My baby ain't been fed in two days.' *Some* said, 'The *only* way we live, Dr. King, is to get food from a neighbor.' And Dr. King started cryin', standin' there in Marks, Mississippi, in what they call the 'Folks' Head-start Program.' And Dr. King started — tears trickled out of his eyes and he said to these people, 'You must have a commitment to something greater than I.' And he preached a sermon about how Hannibal had let man down, how Caesar and even Adolph Hitler, but *God* has never let man down."

Hosea explained some of the many perfidies of the press: "They jumped up and pitted Jesse against Rev. Abernathy. When I came back and everybody knew I was comin' back including Jesse and everybody else, they pitted *me* against Jesse. Then they turned around, and God knows you know what I'm talkin' about, there was a long article on the front page, and they pitted *Hosea* against the marshals. Then they turned around and pitted me against Rev. Abernathy...the news medias are trying to de*stroy* our *leader!* That's what they're tryin' to do."

He concluded by announcing an all-night vigil at the D.C. jail the next evening to await Abernathy's release on Saturday morning. The mule train would be on hand, he said, and Rev. Abernathy would ride in it back across town to the Campaign's Action Center. He said James Bevel would be there to lead the singing and praying during the vigil. He asked those in the church who planned to attend the vigil to stand. Most stood. When they sat down he asked them to stand once more, urging them to stay seated if they didn't mean it. Again, the majority stood.

But most of them really didn't mean it. The vigil was sparsely attended, none of the top staff — including Hosea — were there, and it dwindled nearly away during the night.

By 9:00 A.M., when the crowd was up to a more respectable 200, Mrs. Abernathy arrived to wait with them at the east gate where her husband would be released. A link fence had been set up to keep the crowd away from the jail grounds, but they could still see the cellblock windows in the rear of the five-story building. Campaigners in the cellblock crowded around the windows, shouting "Soul Power!" and waving to the group below, which shouted encouragements in reply.

Abernathy appeared at 9:20, dressed in denims and carrying three huge sacks of mail. He had fasted during his last 17 days in jail and walked very slowly toward the cheering, weeping crowd. A tall black man clambered over the high fence and ran past the guards to help him with the sacks. When he got to the gate he embraced his wife, spoke briefly to the crowd, then got into a station wagon (the mule train being nowhere in sight) and drove off.

At a press conference two hours later he said a statement would be ready on Monday detailing the "new directions" he had decided upon for the Campaign while in jail. After the conference he visited the campsite, which by now had

been completely cleared and almost fully relandscaped. Reporters pressed him for comment, but he seemed a little
shocked by the quiet emptiness of the park, and had little to
say.

It was not hard to guess what these new directions would be.
Most of the staff had already left Washington for a retreat
somewhere to the south. Hosea Williams, in his Deanwood
sermon, had alluded to some changes that might be coming:
"Friends, the Poor People's Campaign is not over. We may
have to shift emphasis but it's not over. God knows I've never
been so tired in my life, but it's not over. They lied upon
us and they cheated, but it's not over. Now we may have to
shift to the convention in Chicago, we may shift some people
to the convention in Miami, we may shift some people into
some o' these Senatorial and Congressional districts where we
can defeat some o' these bigots, but bet your *bottom* dollar,
when Congress open up again, we *will* be back in D.C."
[Applause.]

Such political efforts were the substance of Abernathy's
statement which, as if to maintain one of the Campaign's
traditions, was delayed until Tuesday, July 16. In it he
directed all out-of-town marchers still in the capital "to
return to their homes and join in the local leadership and
activities for poor people," while awaiting "definite assignments from me concerning the campaign on a national level."
He announced plans to visit both national party conventions
with a small group of demonstrators as a delegation from
"the 51st state of hunger." He said he hoped to address both
the platform committees and the assembled delegates, but
promised his group would not try to disrupt the proceedings if
their requests were not granted. A Poor People's Embassy
would be established in Washington to carry on lobbying activities for the poor, and a substantial portion of his time
would be spent working with it. Boycotts were still being considered "against companies which have direct ties to politicians

who have failed to respond to the needs of poor people." The main effort for the fall, however, was to be voter registration drives in certain unnamed marginal House districts where "reactionary members of Congress" could be defeated. Rev. Young added, "We are not just interested in the Black Belt of Alabama . . . but also in some areas of the Midwest and Far West where there are no Negroes."

Abernathy admitted the Campaign had not moved Congress to action on its demands, but claimed nonetheless a "historic victory for poor people" which "dramatically exposed the issue of poverty and will never again permit the nation to ignore it." It "has forced our leading political figures to take a position on the issues of hunger" and "turned away [the nation's attention] from the surface question of violence to the deeper issue of poverty and exploitation that breed violence."

Although Rev. Young did not hesitate to tell the indulgent clergy marchers five days later that "the Poor People's Campaign is not over; it is not even resting," it can hardly be doubted that this press conference marked the Campaign's end. The "New Phase" was little more than a rhetorical smokescreen for a disorderly retreat. "Informed sources" in SCLC indicated there were no concrete plans beyond the visits to the conventions and that it would be some time before any plans were formulated. The ending of the effort was forced on the leadership by the fact that well before Abernathy's release from jail SCLC had lost whatever base in the community it may once have had. No forces were left with which to mount meaningful demonstrations, and the staff — as well, no doubt, as the Administration — knew it. The longer they lingered in Washington, the less credibility as an organization they could hope to salvage.

There was likewise little in the political portions of the "New Phase" that was much different from what SCLC had done before. Dr. King had as a matter of course testified

before platform committees in 1964 and later campaigned in-
dependently for Lyndon Johnson in black communities. The
SCLC staff had been active in several local elections in different areas, such as the campaign to elect black state legis-
lator Carl Stokes mayor of Cleveland. Small-scale boycotts
were likewise nothing new, as we have seen. Only the
projected Poor People's Embassy was a new idea, and it
could hardly be considered a fitting culmination of the summer's effort.

The "New Phase" turned out to be even less substantial
when the election campaigns got underway. The poverty
marchers had no perceptible impact on the GOP's delibera-
tions in Miami, and they went unnoticed in the chaos and
violence surrounding the Democrats' Chicago convulsion.
By late September, when the organization finally got around
to making serious plans for the autumn, its program turned
out to be a repeat of 1964: an unofficial endorsement of Vice
President Humphrey and an all-out drive for a large ghetto
voter turnout in support of the Democratic ticket. No efforts
in marginal Congressional districts ever materialized. The
Poor People's Embassy is still a figure of speech.

Epilogue

If this account of the Poor People's Campaign has a theme, it is that the Campaign never succeeded in bringing about the desired confrontation with the federal government over the issues of poverty and public responsibility. This failure was due at least as much to SCLC's own mistakes as it was to any of the Machiavellian machinations of the Administration and the mass media that Hosea Williams and others saw in every tactical setback and less-than-laudatory news story. This conclusion is the disheartening yet unavoidable result of close, sympathetic observation during the length of the summer program.

It is, of course, much too early to count Dr. King's heirs out as a potent agency of social change, and SCLC still remains a hopeful sign on what is otherwise a pretty bleak national scene.* Still, it will probably be a long time before SCLC will be able to try anything anywhere near as ambitious as the Poor People's Campaign again. The movement left Congress unmoved and possibly even more hostile to the poor. The inefficiency, waste of resources, and other serious internal shortcomings of the organization became painfully visible, major obstacles to its success. All of these alienated a substantial portion of its previous constituency, black *and* white, very likely set back the prospects for a viable multi-ethnic coalition,

*The spring 1969 campaign in Charleston, S. C., was described by Rev. Young as "Part Two of the Poor People's Campaign." But it makes more sense to this writer when it is seen as an effort to rebuild SCLC's credibility and mass support, beginning with its original constituency, an effort made necessary by the Washington Campaign's poor showing.

and weakened by default the credibility of nonviolent change. None of the objectives Martin Luther King hoped to achieve by the Campaign are much nearer: the white backlash is so strong that both presidential candidates pandered to it; the cities are still sliding toward self-strangulation or guerilla war; and in Vietnam, despite diplomatic and political maneuvering, our young men, our wealth, and our remaining integrity are still being steadily devoured. The national situation is if anything more serious today than when Dr. King conceived his "last, greatest dream"; but now we have lost him, his dream has dissipated and the failure of the Poor People's Campaign has left us without an answer to the question that he made the subtitle of his last book: Where do we go from here?